GOD'S PEOPLE IN CHRIST

OVERTURES TO BIBLICAL THEOLOGY
A series of studies in biblical theology designed
to explore fresh dimensions of research and to
suggest ways in which the biblical heritage may
address contemporary culture

Editors

WALTER BRUEGGEMANN, Dean of Academic
Affairs and Professor of Old Testament at
Eden Theological Seminary

JOHN R. DONAHUE, S.J., Associate Professor of
New Testament at Vanderbilt Divinity School

New Testament
Perspectives
on the
Church and
Judaism

GOD'S
PEOPLE
IN CHRIST

DANIEL J. HARRINGTON, S.J.

FORTRESS PRESS   Philadelphia

Library of Congress Cataloging in Publication Data

Harrington, Daniel J
  God's people in Christ.

  (Overtures to Biblical theology)
  Bibliography: p.
  Includes indexes.
  1. Church—Biblical teaching. 2. People of
God—Biblical teaching. 3. Bible. N.T.—Relation
to the Old Testament. I. Title. II. Series.
BS2545.C5H37   262'.7   79–7380
ISBN 0–8006–1531–X

7701E79   Printed in the United States of America   1–1531

To My Parents—God's People in Christ

Contents

Series Foreword

Biblical theology has been a significant part of modern study of the Jewish and Christian Scriptures. Prior to the ascendancy of historical criticism of the Bible in the nineteenth century, biblical theology was subordinated to the dogmatic concerns of the churches, and the Bible too often provided a storehouse of rigid proof texts. When biblical theology was cut loose from its moorings to dogmatic theology to become an enterprise seeking its own methods and categories, attention was directed to what the Bible itself had to say. A dogmatic concern was replaced by an historical one so that biblical theology was understood as an investigation of what was believed by different communities in different situations. By the end of the nineteenth century biblical theology was virtually equated with the history of the religion of the authors who produced biblical documents or of the communities which used them.

While these earlier perspectives have become more refined and sophisticated, they still describe the parameters of what is done in the name of biblical theology—moving somewhere between the normative statements of dogmatic theology and the descriptive concerns of the history of religions. Th. Vriezen, in his *An Outline of Old Testament Theology* (Dutch, 1949; ET, 1958), sought to combine these concerns by devoting the first half of his book to historical considerations and the second half to theological themes. But even that effort did not break out of the stalemate of categories. In more recent times Old Testament theology has been dominated by two paradigmatic works.

In his *Theology of the Old Testament* (German, 1933–39; ET, 1967) W. Eichrodt has provided a comprehensive statement around fixed categories which reflect classical dogmatic interests, although the centrality of covenant in his work reflects the Bible's own categories. By contrast, G. von Rad in his *Old Testament Theology* (German, 1960; ET, 1965) has presented a study of theological traditions with a primary concern for the historical dynamism of the traditions. In the case of New Testament theology, historical and theological concerns are rather roughly juxtaposed in the work of A. Richardson, *An Introduction to the Theology of the New Testament*. As in the case of the Old Testament there are two major options or presentations which dominate in New Testament studies. The history-of-religion school has left its mark on the magisterial work of R. Bultmann, who proceeds from an explanation of the expressions of faith of the earliest communities and their theologians to a statement of how their understanding of existence under faith speaks to us today. The works of O. Cullmann and W. G. Kümmel are clear New Testament statements of *Heilsgeschichte* under the aegis of the tension between promise and fulfillment—categories reminiscent of von Rad.

As recently as 1962 K. Stendahl again underscored the tension between historical description and normative meaning by assigning to the biblical theologian the task of describing what the Bible *meant,* not what it *means* or *how* it can have meaning. However, this objectivity of historical description is too often found to be a mirror of the observer's hidden preunderstanding, and the adequacy of historical description is contingent on one generation's discoveries and postulates. Also, the yearning and expectation of believers and would-be believers will not let biblical theology rest with the descriptive task alone. The growing strength of Evangelical Protestantism and the expanding phenomenon of charismatic Catholicism are but vocal reminders that people seek in the Bible a source of alternative value systems. By its own character and by the place it occupies in our culture the Bible will not rest easy as merely an historical artifact.

Thus it seems a fitting time to make "overtures" concerning biblical theology. It is not a time for massive tomes which claim too much. It appears not even to be a time for firm conclusions which are too comprehensive. It is a time for pursuit of fresh hints, for exploration of new intuitions which may reach beyond old conclusions, set categories, and conventional methods. The books in this series are concerned not only with what is seen and heard, with what the Bible said, but also with what the Bible says and the ways in which seeing and hearing are done.

In putting forth these *Overtures* much remains unsettled. The certainties of the older biblical theology *in service* of dogmatics, as well as of the more recent biblical theology movement *in lieu* of dogmatics, are no longer present. Nor is there on the scene anyone of the stature of a von Rad or a Bultmann to offer a synthesis which commands the theological engagement of a generation and summons the church to a new restatement of the biblical message. In a period characterized by an information explosion the relation of analytic study to attempts at synthesis is unsettled. Also unsettled is the question whether the scholarly canon of the university or the passion of the confessing community provides a language and idiom of discourse, and equally unsettled—and unsettling—is the question whether biblical theology is simply one more specialization in an already fragmented study of Scripture or whether it is finally the point of it all.

But much remains clear. Not simply must the community of biblical scholars address fresh issues and articulate new categories for the well-being of our common professional task; equally urgent is the fact that the dominant intellectual tradition of the West seems now to carry less conviction and to satisfy only weakly the new measures of knowing which are among us. We do not know exactly what role the Bible will play in new theological statements or religious postures, nor what questions the Bible can and will address, but *Overtures* will provide a locus where soundings may be taken.

We not only intend that *Overtures* should make contact with people professionally involved in biblical studies, but hope that the series will speak to all who care about the heritage of the biblical tradition. We hope that the volumes will represent the best in a literary and historical study of biblical traditions without canonizing historical archaism. We hope also that the studies will be relevant without losing the mystery of biblical religion's historical distance, and that the studies touch on significant themes, motifs, and symbols of the Bible without losing the rich diversity of the biblical tradition. It is a time for normative literature which is not heavy-handed, but which seriously challenges not only our conclusions but also the shape of our questions.

God's People in Christ treats a subject which is of concern not simply to the contemporary reader of the Bible but which has addressed the Christian church from its inception and throughout its existence—the relation of the church to its parent, the people of Israel. While the work is an overture primarily for Christians to rediscover their Jewish roots, not only in the Old Testament but in all the major portions of the New Testament, it also invites Jewish readers to see how a scholar who is most conversant in the Hebrew Bible and in the Jewish literature of the first century of our era pictures the relation of Christian faith, in its earliest stages, to its Jewish matrix.

Much of the best work in contemporary New Testament exegesis and in the presentation of its results to nonspecialists consists in helping readers to see familiar texts in a new light. Harrington's work is an invitation to such an experience. After discussing the roots of the early communities in postexilic Judaism, the author guides the reader through major blocks of the New Testament. The book should be read with New Testament at hand. The presentation of the material embraces two major emphases. One is a careful picture of how the early church viewed itself in relation to the events of the life, death, and resurrection of Jesus, so that the book offers in effect a succinct and evocative study of New Testament ecclesiology. The other emphasis is to describe how this identity was forged in relation to Judaism and to catalog the stages by which early Christian communities began to emerge as distinct religious groupings and no longer as a part of Judaism. Harrington's picture of the relation of unity and diversity in early Christians' understanding of themselves as God's people helps us to address an important current question: What does it mean to be a member of a *Christian* community? Of equal import, his work helps us to respond to another question: Can one be a Christian without affirming a vital link with Judaism?

Daniel J. Harrington, S.J., is a Professor of New Testament at the Weston School of Theology (Cambridge, Mass.). He is known for his technical scholarship on the Biblical Antiquities of Pseudo-Philo, a work roughly contemporaneous with the origin of Christianity. He has also written extensively on New Testament understandings of church and on other aspects of New Testament theology. His position as editor of *New Testament Abstracts* makes him uniquely familiar with the vast amount of material published on the New Testament. The chapters of *God's People in Christ* offer the reader an appropriation and representation of much of what is best in contemporary scholarship on the church in the New Testament.

WALTER BRUEGGEMANN
JOHN R. DONAHUE, S.J.

Abbreviations

AB	Anchor Bible
AUSS	*Andrews University Seminary Studies*
BA	*Biblical Archaeologist*
BETL	Bibliotheca Ephemeridum Theologicarum Lovaniensium
BGBE	Beiträge zur Geschichte der biblischen Exegese
BTB	*Biblical Theology Bulletin*
CBQ	*Catholic Biblical Quarterly*
CurTM	*Currents in Theology and Mission*
ExpTim	*Expository Times*
FRLANT	Forschungen zur Religion und Literatur des Alten und Neuen Testaments
HeyJ	*Heythrop Journal*
HNT	Handbuch zum Neuen Testament
HR	*History of Religions*
Int	*Interpretation*
JBL	*Journal of Biblical Literature*
LD	Lectio Divina
NovT	*Novum Testamentum*
NovTSup	Novum Testamentum, Supplements
NTAbh	Neutestamentliche Abhandlungen
NTS	*New Testament Studies*
RB	*Revue Biblique*
SANT	Studien zum Alten und Neuen Testament
SBLDS	SBL Dissertation Series
SBLSCS	SBL Septuagint and Cognate Studies

SBT	Studies in Biblical Theology
ScEs	*Science et esprit*
SNTSMS	Society for New Testament Studies Monograph Series
ST	*Studia theologica*
TD	*Theology Digest*
TLZ	*Theologische Literaturzeitung*
TQ	*Theologische Quartalschrift*
TS	*Theological Studies*
USQR	*Union Seminary Quarterly Review*
ZKT	*Zeitschrift für katholische Theologie*

Preface

It has become common in recent times for Christians to refer to the church as the people of God. This small study explores the biblical foundations for this title and the special relationship with God it implies and points out the challenges that the relevant scriptural texts present to the church today. It is written primarily with theological students and interested church members in mind. The description of the church as the people of God is also a sensitive and controversial topic in discussions between Jewish theologians and Christian theologians, and this presentation of the biblical evidence for the Christian claim to be God's people is intended as a contribution to such conversations.

The study is an exercise in biblical theology. It focuses on specific texts and tries to listen to what these texts said in their original settings and what they may be saying to the church today. Readers may need to refer to a text of the Bible at some points, though I have quoted from the Revised Standard Version where I thought it to be necessary. Not every biblical text that touches on the theme of the church as the people of God has been cited, but enough exegetical material is supplied to let the reader see how other passages could be integrated into an understanding of the church as God's people in Christ.

My basic thesis is that the church's claim to be God's people rests entirely on the person of Jesus Christ. If there is any single New Testament text that summarizes my position, it is Gal. 3:29: "If you are Christ's, then you are Abraham's offspring, heirs according to promise." The application of the title "people of God" to the church challenges it to reflect on the bonds that exist between Christians and on its debt to and present relationship with Judaism. I gratefully acknowledge the receipt of a grant from the Association of Theological Schools for the academic year 1978–79. I also express gratitude to my students at the Weston School of Theology in Cambridge, Mass., and to members of other church groups who have helped me to refine my ideas on this topic. But my greatest debt of gratitude is reserved for my parents, who have showed me over many years what it means to be part of God's people in Christ.

DANIEL J. HARRINGTON, S.J.

Weston School of Theology

CHAPTER 1

Problems and
Possibilities

Recent writings on ecclesiology, especially in Roman Catholic circles since the Second Vatican Council, place a strong emphasis on the church as the people of God.[1] The theological premise on which this identification is based is that insofar as Christ has fulfilled the hopes of the Old Testament people of God, those now gathered around him (whether they be of Jewish or Gentile origin) constitute the true people of God.[2] Conversely, from a Christian perspective the church is seen to have been given the prerogatives of the Old Testament people of God and is challenged to remain faithful to Israel's divinely initiated, historical, and covenantal structure of faith.

The description of the church as the people of God has become popular for some very good reasons. It underlines the continuity between the Israel of the Old Testament and the church of the New Testament. It preserves a communitarian dimension for the church and avoids an unhealthy overemphasis on leaders and offices. It captures the historical, "on-the-move" character of the church and rescues it from lifeless and static thinking. Nevertheless, in some circles *people of God* threatens to become a kind of ecclesiastical buzzword—one that inspires interest and positive response but whose meaning remains somewhat elusive. Those who are fond of using the term should be reminded that only in 1 Pet. 2:10 is the Christian community unequivocally and explicitly addressed as the people of God ("now you are God's people")—and even there only after a series of allusions to the Old Testament titles of

1

Israel in the preceding verse.[3] This identification of the church as the people of God may be in the background of many New Testament documents, but it is seldom made explicit. The earliest Christians were apparently a bit hesitant about drawing what may seem to us only a logical conclusion.[4] Perhaps their diffidence on this matter indicates that the idea of the church as the people of God is more complicated than it may seem on the surface and that the biblical foundation for this identification needs more exploration than it is usually given.

A BIBLICAL-THEOLOGICAL STUDY

This book is a biblical-theological study of the church as the people of God. Taking its leads from relevant scriptural texts, it is designed to assist church people to understand more profoundly the implications of the phrase that they may have used casually and without much reflection. Study of this topic gives us insight into the primary pastoral problem confronting the early church: By what right do those not born Jewish belong to the people of God? It also reveals the ways in which various Christian writers of the first century struggled with the problem of the church's continuity with Israel as God's people. It sensitizes us to the major questions arising in modern dialogues between Jews and Christians: How can the church call itself the people of God? Why does no New Testament writer describe the church as "the true Israel" or "the new Israel"? What is the historical setting of the blatantly "anti-Jewish" statements in the New Testament? Finally, it provides us with a renewed appreciation for the centrality of Christ and the importance of baptism in Christian faith.

The topic of the church as the people of God has broad significance. It has become a popular description of the church today and touches on important issues in New Testament times and Christian theology. Nevertheless, any attempt at a professedly biblical-theological study of this topic soon encounters genuine difficulties brought about by our increased understanding of the biblical documents themselves.[5] There are divergent theological outlooks within the Bible. The four Gospels attempting to portray the one Jesus illustrate this point. They exhibit important differences in the order, selection, and presentation of material about Jesus. Matthew's portrait of Christ differs from Luke's, and so on. Moreover, the New Testament writings spoke primarily and directly to the people and situations of the first century A.D. in various places of the Mediterranean world. So much of our construction of later Christianity really depends, for example, on the ways in which Paul dealt with specific problems confronting the churches at Corinth or Thessalonica. Nineteen hundred years of human history separate us from those situations, and the question naturally arises as to the amount of transfer-value that we can allow these texts. Lastly, the canon of Scripture itself represents only a selection of witnesses to early Christianity. Obviously the canon took shape after the documents had circulated for some time. Defense against gnosticism, sanctifying books already familiar in church usage, and presumption of apostolic authorship were among the reasons for including books within the canon. We know the voices of Paul's opponents only from his replies to their excesses (as in Galatians and 1 Corinthians), and the letter to the Laodiceans mentioned in Col. 4:16 seems to have vanished.

These problems—the divergent theological outlooks, the historical conditioning of the documents, and the selective character of the canon—present serious obstacles to anyone who would attempt a biblical-theological study. Indeed, the combination of them has led many New Testament specialists to give up entirely on the enterprise of biblical theology. But can the church afford to give up on biblical theology? After all, the church in which we read Scripture and live our religious lives assumes that these documents, for all their historical conditioning, do have a transhistorical significance. The apostolic era has traditionally been viewed as a privileged period in Christian history, and its documents have provided the church throughout the ages with direction, challenge, and criteria for judging itself.

In this study I am not joining all biblical statements about the people of God into one comprehensive doctrine of the church, and I am not suggesting that there is only one pattern for the church in the New Testament. On the other hand, I am not treating the New Testament documents solely as historical curiosities from antiquity whose meaning is exhausted when they are understood in their original setting. Rather, I will try to be as faithful as possible to the original meaning and historical setting of the particular texts studied here while pointing out what I perceive to be their abiding significance for the church. The task is primarily descriptive and historical, but the church's long tradition of reading the Bible affirms that this description and this history have significance for us today.

ANCIENT ISRAEL'S CONSCIOUSNESS OF ITSELF AS A PEOPLE

A study primarily concerned with the church as the people of God according to the New Testament cannot explore in depth the historical development of ancient Israel's consciousness of itself as a people.[6] Yet the basic structure of Israel's relationship with Yahweh has significance for the life of the church, and the topic can hardly be ignored. A compromise solution to this quandary is to rely on some evocative Old Testament texts that will illustrate the divinely initiated, historical, and covenantal character of that relationship and its challenges for the church.

In Gen. 12:1–3 God's first words to Abraham promise the gift of the land and assure a great posterity:

> [1] Now the Lord said to Abram, "Go from your country and your kindred and your father's house to the land that I will show you. [2] And I will make of you a great nation, and I will bless you, and make your name great, so that you will be a blessing. [3] I will bless those who bless you, and him who curses you I will curse; and by you all the families of the earth shall bless themselves."

The history of salvation begins with God's call to Abraham and through Abraham to his descendants. After the chaos described in the first eleven chapters of Genesis, the initiative of God sets into motion the story of the people of Israel. Far from being simply the story of an individual and his exploits, the Abraham narratives are significant because they tell the tale of a people's beginnings. It is God's fidelity that will make of these nomads a people. The concluding part of the promise to Abraham (v. 3) insists on Israel's special status with respect to the other peoples of the earth. Because the God of Israel is the lord of human history, he will bless those who bless Israel and curse those who curse Israel. Thus Gen. 12:1–3 contains in a brief compass many features characteristic of Israel's sense of peoplehood: the divine initiative, the communal nature of salvation, the central significance of God's fidelity and the gift of the land, and the place of Israel with reference to other peoples.

Another important Old Testament text expressing the dimensions of Israel's recognition of itself as God's people is the ancient liturgical confession found in Deut. 26:5–11:

> 5 "And you shall make response before the Lord your God, 'A wandering Aramean was my father; and he went down into Egypt and sojourned there, few in number; and there he became a nation, great, mighty, and populous. 6 And the Egyptians treated us harshly, and afflicted us, and laid upon us hard bondage. 7 Then we cried to the Lord the God of our fathers, and the Lord heard our voice, and saw our affliction, our toil, and our oppression; 8 and the Lord brought us out of Egypt with a mighty hand and an outstretched arm, with great terror, with signs and wonders; 9 and he brought us into this place and gave us this land, a land flowing with milk and honey. 10 And behold, now I bring the first of the fruit of the ground, which thou, O Lord, hast given me.' And you shall set it down before the Lord your God, and worship before the Lord your God; 11 and you shall rejoice in all the good which the Lord God has given to you and to your house, you, and the Levite, and the sojourner who is among you."

The offering of the firstfruits described in vv. 10–11 connects the passage with the festival of weeks (Pentecost), originally an old Canaanite agricultural celebration but now in this text reinterpreted in the light of Israel's history. As a liturgical confession the text obviously is older than the document in which it now appears, and it reflects the beliefs of the community as a whole. The confession summarizes Israel's history from the journey of the patriarch Jacob ("a wandering Aramean was my father") into Egypt in order to escape famine, through the persecution of Israel in Egypt, to the escape from Egypt and the gift of the land of Canaan. Israel's response to the harsh treatment by the Egyptians was petition to "the God of our fathers" (v. 7)—a response indicative of Israel's belief that its God does hear prayers and does intervene in history. The two mighty acts of God that are singled out for special praise are the Exodus and the bestowal of the land. Thus the offering of the firstfruits is a symbolic acknowledgment of God's gracious activity in which the Israelite gives back a share of the crops to the giver of all good gifts. In this liturgical confession Israel recognizes itself as a people gifted by God, especially in the Exodus and the entrance into the land of Canaan. It sees its history as the record of an encounter with Yahweh and a response to that encounter.

A similar emphasis on Israel's knowledge of God as derived from reflection on its history can be glimpsed in Psalm 98. The last few lines of the psalm (vv. 7–9) with their references to water and the coming of Yahweh as king and judge connect it to the enthronement festival thought to have been celebrated in the autumn. Autumn marks the beginning of the life-giving rains in Israel, and their appearance or nonappearance was attributed to divine forces in the ancient Near East. So the connection drawn in the psalm between the rains and Yahweh is entirely intelligible. But if one looks at the first three verses of the psalm, one sees that the appeal is to Yahweh's historical activity on behalf of Israel, not to his activity in nature:

> ¹ O sing to the Lord a new song,
>   for he has done marvelous things!
> His right hand and his holy arm have gotten him victory.
> ² The Lord has made known his victory,
>   he has revealed his vindication in the sight of the nations.
> ³ He has remembered his steadfast love and faithfulness
>   to the house of Israel.
> All the ends of the earth have seen
>   the victory of our God.

Yahweh the warrior is celebrated. In its battles Israel has experienced Yahweh's right hand and holy arm (see Deut. 26:8) as powerful against its foes (v. 1). God's activity on behalf of his people has been revealed to the other nations (v. 2), and his loyalty to the covenant ("steadfast love and faithfulness") has been made known to Israel. This psalm celebrating Yahweh's past exploits in war and in nature and looking forward to his coming as judge rests on the same assumption as Deut. 26:5–11: God shows his favor toward Israel as a people in his gracious direction of history, and he acts on behalf of Israel because he is faithful to his covenant.

Mention of the covenant brings us to the passage that recounts the constitution of Israel as an alliance of twelve tribes— the covenant at Shechem described in Joshua 24. After Moses' death, Joshua leads the people into the land of Canaan and now as his final act of leadership assembles the tribes of Israel at Shechem for a covenant ceremony. The first part of the discourse is a rehearsal of Yahweh's deeds on behalf of his people from the patriarchs (vv. 2–4), through the Exodus (vv. 5–7) and the battles with the kings on the other side of the Jordan (vv. 8–10), to the gift of the land (vv. 11–13). Yahweh has proved himself as God in his mighty acts, and now Israel is challenged to fear him and serve him:

> [14] "Now therefore fear the Lord, and serve him in sincerity and in faithfulness; put away the gods which your fathers served beyond the River, and in Egypt, and serve the Lord. [15] And if you be unwilling to serve the Lord, choose this day whom you will serve, whether the gods your fathers served in the region beyond the River, or the gods of the Amorites in whose land you dwell; but as for me and my house, we will serve the Lord."

The covenant concept derives from agreements between masters (suzerains) and servant chiefs (vassals). The summons to "fear" in the context of the covenant ceremony refers to the respect or awe due to the master from the servant and is based on an accurate assessment of who God is. "Serve" refers to the decision to enter the covenantal relationship existing between master and servant. Challenged to fear the Lord and serve him

(v. 14), the tribes affirm their willingness to respond to God's gracious initiatives (vv. 18, 21, 24). This response involves putting away all other lords and observing the "statutes and ordinances" (v. 25) that constitute the covenant obligations. In the ceremony at Shechem Israel emerges as an association of tribes that has accepted as the basis of its common life the worship of Yahweh alone and has made a covenant to that effect.[7] God's saving action in the Exodus and his gift of the land provide the historical grounds for why Israel should enter into covenant relationship. The covenant relationship in turn furnishes a religious context for the observance of the Law as the revelation of the divine will. What makes the twelve tribes into a people is Yahweh's presence as God, the possession of the land promised to Israel, and the observance of the covenant stipulations as God's Law.

The threat posed by the Philistine invasions in the middle of the eleventh century B.C. could not be met by the loose confederation of tribes formed in Joshua 24. Though kingship brought some unfortunate theological and political consequences (see 1 Sam. 8:4–22), the building of the Davidic monarchy was integrated into Israel's covenant traditions and viewed as yet another instance of Yahweh's care for his people. Nathan's oracle to David (2 Sam. 7:12–16) assures that Israel's royal line will last:

> [12] " 'When your days are fulfilled and you lie down with your fathers, I will raise up your son after you, who shall come forth from your body, and I will establish his kingdom. [13] He shall build a house for my name, and I will establish the throne of his kingdom for ever. [14] I will be his father, and he shall be my son. When he commits iniquity, I will chasten him with the rod of men, with the stripes of the sons of men; [15] but I will not take my steadfast love from him, as I took it from Saul, whom I put away from before you. [16] And your house and your kingdom shall be made sure for ever before me; your throne shall be established for ever.' "

Though individual kings will be punished for their breaches of the covenant stipulations (v. 14), Yahweh's love will not be taken away (v. 15). The great prophets preached that God could and would hand his people over to subjection because of its sins. Nevertheless, they too insisted on the eternal character of God's covenant love and urged a return to perfect observance of the covenant (e.g. Jer. 3:12–13; 31:31–34). In Isaiah 40—55 restoration of Israel's relationship with God is presented in terms of a new creation and a new exodus, and the traditional elements of Israel's peoplehood (God, land, and Law) are reemphasized.

Perhaps no text better summarizes Israel's peculiar consciousness of itself as a people than Deut. 7:6–9:

> [6] "For you are a people holy to the Lord your God; the Lord your God has chosen you to be a people for his own possession, out of all the peoples that are on the face of the earth. [7] It was not because you were more in number than any other people that the Lord set his love upon you and chose you, for you were the fewest of all peoples; [8] but it is because the Lord loves you, and is keeping the oath which he swore to your fathers, that the Lord has brought you out with a mighty hand, and redeemed you from the house of bondage, from the hand of Pharaoh king of Egypt. [9] Know therefore that the Lord your God is God, the faithful God who keeps covenant and steadfast love with those who love him and keep his commandments, to a thousand generations."

The issue here is the source of Israel's status as God's people. Is Israel's understanding of itself the kind of crude nationalism or racism that has repeatedly appeared in human history? Or is it something else? Some now-familiar features in Israel's self-consciousness recur in this passage: the divine initiative in the choice of Israel (v. 6), the communal nature of salvation (v. 6), God's fidelity to Israel in its past history (v. 8), the utter gratuity of Israel's election (v. 7), and the covenantal nature of the relationship between Yahweh and Israel (v. 9). Israel's election emerges as a divine prerogative. Rather than being based on its alleged superiority to other peoples, Israel's special status depends entirely on God's grace. Consciousness of its role as God's people furnishes the context in which observance of the Law is a response to God's initiatives. Throughout the Old Testament Israel's picture of itself is unflatteringly honest with little hesitation about describing the sins of its heroes and its sins as a people. Its election is a vocational one in that Israel must serve the Lord of the covenant and (in some parts of the Old Testament, e.g. Isa. 42:6) must be a light to other peoples. All these features set Israel's recognition of itself as God's people far apart from any crude nationalism or racism.

AFTER THE EXILE

With the restoration of the temple and the renewal of Judaism under Ezra and Nehemiah, Israel's awareness of itself as God's people and as being in covenant relationship with him remained the major theme. But many writings from the Second Temple period show a tendency toward specifying or concretizing the covenant relationship by focusing on particular commandments. Emphasis may be placed on marriage within the Jewish community, circumcision, keeping the Sabbath, belonging to the "right" religious group, or worshiping the God of Israel and him alone. In the cosmopolitan atmosphere of Hellenism and in view of Israel's subject status within the Persian, Ptolemaic, Seleucid, and Roman empires successively, such emphases constituted effective and concrete means of preserving the distinctive character of the Jewish heritage. They should not be hastily dismissed as instances of Jewish "legalism."[8]

On his arrival in Jerusalem Ezra insisted that the Israelites there give up their foreign spouses (Ezra 9—10) presumably on the assumption that intermarriage is a serious threat to the true relationship between Yahweh and his people. In the "praise of famous men" in Ecclesiasticus 44—50, Ben Sira takes up the theme of Abraham as the father of many nations (44:19-21) and focuses on circumcision ("he established the covenant in his flesh") at a time when circumcision was increasingly viewed as the distinguishing mark of Jewish males (see 1 Macc. 1:11–15). The Lord made Abraham the father of many nations because he kept the Law, because he entered into the covenant of circumcision, and because he was found faithful in testing. In Bk. Jub. 2:31–32 God is said to have given to Israel the privilege of observing the Sabbath: "He did not sanctify all peoples and nations to keep the Sabbath on it [the seventh day], but Israel alone; them alone he permitted to eat and drink and to keep the Sabbath on it on the earth." The Essene community that gave us the Dead Sea scrolls from the region around Qumran stressed the importance of belonging to its movement. Convinced that those who controlled the Jerusalem temple had gone astray, the Qumran community narrowed down "the covenant of grace" (Rule of the Community 1:8) to members of "the community of God" (1:12). The community appropriated to itself the epithets traditionally applied to the temple: house of holiness, company of infinite holiness for Aaron, an everlasting planting, the precious cornerstone, the dwelling of infinite holiness, and the house of perfection and truth in Israel (Rule of the Community 8:5–10).

Pseudo-Philo's Biblical Antiquities, which was most likely written in Palestine around the time of Jesus and is a precious source for understanding how the Bible was being interpreted in that period, displays a strong interest in Israel as God's people and in the covenant. For example, the holy land is said not to have been touched by the flood (7:4). The people of Israel cannot be destroyed as long as the world exists (9:3) and can be defeated only if they sin (18:13). Israel is the vine of God (12:8; 18:10; 23:11–12; 28:4; 30:4; 39:7) and the flock of God (23:12; 32:5). In fact, if God were to destroy Israel, there would be no one to glorify him (12:9). At the root of the author's views on God and humanity is the general notion of the covenant with Israel, but idolatry and mixed marriages are singled out as the most reprehensible sins against the Law. Abraham would rather have died than take part in idolatrous rites (chap. 6), but the people of Israel were repeatedly led astray after false gods (chaps. 25; 34; 36; 38; 44). Intercourse and marriage with Gentiles are roundly condemned in 9:1, 5; 18:13–14; 21:1; 30:1; 43:5; 44:7; 45:3.

In all these Jewish writings from the so-called postexilic or intertestamental periods the biblical pattern of election and covenant is assumed, but special emphasis is placed on particular commandments (prohibition of mixed marriages, circumcision of males, observance of the Sabbath, belonging to the proper group, worship of Yahweh alone) that would insure consciousness of belonging to God's people in a cosmopolitan milieu.

DEVELOPMENTS IN THE NEW TESTAMENT

We have explored some of the fundamental dimensions of Israel's recognition of itself as God's people and traced the postexilic tendency to specify or concretize that relationship by emphasis on one or several commandments. Those Israelites who avoid intermarriage or breaking the Sabbath or apostasy constitute God's people. Those Israelites who practice circumcision or have nothing to do with evildoers are God's chosen ones. Within this context of Israel's covenant relationship with God, the early church offered its claim to be "God's people" (1 Pet. 2:10) on the basis of the confession that Jesus of Nazareth is the Messiah of Israel. But even within the relatively narrow confines of the New Testament canon this claim is far from being univocal. The remainder of this book is concerned with investigating the various ways in which the Christian claims to be God's people are made in the New Testament and the theological gains and problems that these claims entail.

From Paul's letters in the fifties of the first century A.D. to the books written in the last years of the first century, several differing orientations can be traced. In Galatians 3 Paul insists that one becomes a true child of Abraham and therefore part of God's people through baptism into Christ. Far from being a rejection of or departure from the Old Testament Scriptures, this way of incorporation into God's people is presented as perfectly consistent with those Scriptures and the real purposes of the Law. Then in Romans 9—11, Paul spells out a three-stage process in the history of salvation: (1) While some Israelites like Paul have accepted the gospel, there is a hardening of understanding and of heart in part of Israel. (2) The Gentiles are now being included in the people of God. When the full number of Gentiles comes in, the hardened part of Israel will become jealous and then accept the gospel. (3) In the end all

Israel will be saved. Paul is very aware of Israel's traditional claim to be the people of God and hesitates to apply that title too facilely to the church (except perhaps "the Israel of God" in Gal. 6:16).

Documents written after the time of the uncontested Pauline epistles show less hesitation in transferring the old Israel's privileges to the church. The letter to the Ephesians speaks of Jews and Gentiles coming together to form one new humanity, one body, and one Spirit (2:11–18). In 1 Peter the tie that binds Christians is said to be so close that they can appropriately be addressed as a race and a people (2:9–10). The author of the letter to the Hebrews urges the church to profit from the bad example of Israel in the wilderness (3:7—4:11). The Book of Revelation addresses Christians as priests of God and of Christ (1:6; 5:10; 20:6). In all these documents the Christian community is portrayed as somehow replacing Israel as God's people, and there is little or no interest in the future fate of "unbelieving" Israel.

The two Gospels that have traditionally been viewed as the most "Jewish" have also been charged with being the most "anti-Jewish" writings in the New Testament. How have the Gospels of Matthew and John gained this paradoxical reputation? When read in their original historical settings of conflict with the Jewish synagogues, the peculiar "Jewish" and "anti-Jewish" character of the Gospels becomes intelligible. After the temple in Jerusalem had been destroyed in A.D. 70 and the efforts at reconstituting Judaism were underway, Christianity came increasingly to be seen as going beyond the boundaries of traditional Judaism and as constituting a new and different religious orientation. According to Matt. 21:43 the privileges of the old Israel have been taken away from the present political and religious leaders and given to the new "nation" that produces fruit (that is, the church). Like Matthew who speaks of "their synagogues" and criticizes the leaders of those synagogues as hypocrites, so John appears to reflect the hostility engendered by the expulsion of Christians from the synagogue. These Gospels go beyond the "replacement" theology of

Ephesians, 1 Peter, Hebrews, and Revelation to a kind of "conflict" theology in which the fate of "unbelieving" Israel is portrayed in very negative hues. Paul's salvation-historical thinking, the replacement theology of the post-Pauline writings, and the conflict theology of the Gospels represent the major developments in the idea of the church as the people of God in the New Testament. Careful attention to each of these orientations may help us to be more circumspect and understanding in our talk of the church as the people of God. But before discussing these matters, we must say something about the relationship between Jesus' preaching of the kingdom of God and the church and about the earliest Christian community in Jerusalem insofar as this can be known from Acts 1—2.

NOTES

1. See the second chapter in Vatican II's Dogmatic Constitution on the Church (*Lumen Gentium*) in *Documents of Vatican II*, ed. W. Abbott (New York: America Press/Guild Press/Association Press, 1966), pp. 24–37. The Greek word for church is *ekklēsia*. Though in the Greek world it referred to a regularly summoned political body and had no religious connotation, the Greek version of the Old Testament used it to describe the congregation of Israelites chosen by God and gathered around him for religious purposes. In the New Testament *ekklēsia* can refer to the local Christian community (the far more common usage) or to the universal church to which all believers belong (especially in the letter to the Ephesians). The repeated use of the term *the church* in the course of this study probably reflects my Roman Catholic heritage. Those who come from other Christian traditions can easily substitute terms more familiar to them, e.g. *the community* or *the early church*.

2. A. Jaubert, "D'Israël à l'Église," *Quatre Fleuves* 5 (1975): 4–13.

3. J.-M. Leonard, "Invitation à la prudence dans l'emploi de l'expression 'Peuple de Dieu,'" *Communio Viatorum* 19 (1976): 35–60.

4. P. Richardson, *Israel in the Apostolic Church*, SNTSMS 10 (New York: Cambridge University Press, 1970).

5. D. J. Harrington, "Ernst Käsemann's Understanding of the Church in the New Testament," *HeyJ* 12 (1971): 246–57, 367–78.

6. N. A. Dahl, *Das Volk Gottes: Eine Untersuchung zum Kirchenbewusstsein des Urchristentums* (Oslo: Jacob Dybwad, 1941).

7. H. J. Kraus, *The People of God in the Old Testament* (New York and London: Association Press, 1958), p. 12. See also E. Galbiati, "La funzione d'Israele nella 'economia' della salvezza," *Bibbia e Oriente* 20 (1978): 5–16.

8. C. Klein, *Anti-Judaism in Christian Theology*, trans. E. Quinn (Philadelphia: Fortress Press, 1978). See now G. Baumbach, " 'Volk Gottes' im Frühjudentum. Eine Untersuchung der 'ekklesiologischen' Typen des Frühjudentums," *Kairos* 21 (1979): 30–47. According to Baumbach, three general attitudes toward who constitutes the people of God may be distinguished among Jews of Jesus' time: spiritualistic-universal (radical Hellenizers, moderate reformers like Philo), particularistic-hierocratic (Maccabeans, Sadducees), and pietistic-nomistic (Hasideans, Essenes, Pharisees).

CHAPTER 2

Kingdom and Church
in Jesus' Preaching

If we wish to understand the New Testament church as the people of God in Christ, we must first make an honest effort to relate that church to the teaching and person of Jesus himself. Even a cursory reading of the synoptic Gospels will show that the most important theme of Jesus' preaching was the kingdom of God. So pervasive was the motif of the kingdom in the Jewish theology at the time of Jesus that it apparently needed little explanation. Yet few concepts have been so misunderstood throughout the church's history. The kingdom of God has been wrongly identified as the soul of the individual Christian, the earthly kingdom, or the church. Church leaders and even learned theologians speak incorrectly about our building up the kingdom of God.[1] Three questions will concern us in this chapter: How was the kingdom of God understood in the Judaism of Jesus' time? What were the dimensions of Jesus' own teaching about the kingdom? Did Jesus found a church? Though these questions do not directly develop our major theme of the church as the people of God, their importance for New Testament ecclesiology in general is such that they can scarcely be avoided at this point.

THE KINGDOM OF GOD IN JUDAISM

The kingdom of God refers to God's future display of power and judgment and to the eventual establishment of his rule over all creation. At that time all creation will acknowledge the God of Israel as the only God and the only Lord. Obviously this

17

idea has roots in the Old Testament doctrine of God's kingship over all creation (see Psalm 98) and the promises of an eternal kingship for Israel (see 2 Sam. 7:12–16). But it is not precisely the same thing. The Old Testament kind of kingship is assumed, but the doctrine of the kingdom of God in Jesus' time was concerned more with that point in the future when God's kingship will become more manifest than ever. It is primarily an eschatological concept; that is, it refers to the last day in human history as we know it before the new divine order is established. This doctrine of the eschatological kingdom of God was the most important theological teaching of Judaism in Jesus' time. What we have of Jesus' teaching in the synoptic Gospels is absolutely incomprehensible without it, and it also provided the theological framework for early Christian writers when they sought to express their beliefs about Jesus and his significance.

The so-called Apocalypse of Weeks in 1 Enoch illustrates what at least some Jews around Jesus' time thought about the kingdom of God. According to Gen. 5:22–24 Enoch was taken up into heaven, and in the Judaism of Jesus' time he was understood as one who took heavenly journeys and was granted secret knowledge. The Apocalypse of Weeks appears in a collection or anthology of Jewish writings connected with the figure of Enoch. Fragments of it have been found at Qumran.[2] The Apocalypse recounts a vision in which ten weeks or historical periods are unfolded. The first seven weeks tell of events that are past from the reader's perspective (Adam to Enoch, Enoch to the flood, Abraham, Moses, building the temple, the monarchy to the Exile, return from exile to the second century B.C.) and prepare for this description of the future kingdom in the last three weeks in 1 Enoch 91:12–17:

> [12] And after that there shall be another, the eighth week, that
>   of righteousness,
>   And a sword shall be given to it that a righteous judgment
>   may be executed on the oppressors,
>   And sinners shall be delivered into the hands of the
>   righteous.

13 And at its close they shall acquire houses through their
righteousness,
And a house shall be built for the Great King in glory for
evermore,
And all mankind shall look to the path of uprightness.

14 And after that, in the ninth week, the righteous judgment
shall be revealed to the whole world,
And all the works of the godless shall vanish from all the
earth,
And the world shall be written down for destruction.

15 And after this, in the tenth week in the seventh part,
There shall be the great eternal judgment,
In which He will execute vengeance amongst the angels.

16 And the first heaven shall depart and pass away,
And a new heaven shall appear,
And all the powers of the heavens shall give sevenfold light.

17 And after that there will be many weeks without number
for ever,
And all shall be in goodness and righteousness,
And sin shall no more be mentioned for ever.

(R. H. Charles)

The eighth week (91:12–13) describes the establishing of
righteousness in Israel. A military action under divine initiative
("a sword shall be given to it") is envisioned in which op-
pressors (political leaders) and sinners (impious Jews) will be
delivered into the hands of the righteous (the author and his
community). The righteous will acquire power and build a
proper temple ("a house for the great king"), and a new age
of righteousness will begin in Israel. In the ninth week (91:14)
the focus is broadened to include the whole world. Then all the
world will see the righteous judgments of God, and his Law
will be extended to all nations and peoples. Evil and the world
of evil will be destroyed. The tenth week (91:15–17) will see
God's vengeance on the evil angels (see 1 Enoch 6—11 for the
angel's rebellion as the "original sin"), the disappearance of

the "first" heaven and the appearance of the new heaven, and the coming of the eternal kingdom of God in which goodness and righteousness will prevail and sin will have no place.

What then does the Apocalypse of Weeks tell us about the kingdom of God? The primary actor is God himself. Though indirect speech and passive verbs abound, there is no real doubt as to who is in charge. God initiates the military actions on earth and executes the judgment in heaven. The events are going to occur in the future. Many important religious traditions of ancient Israel (the decisive significance of observing the Law, the temple, the Day of the Lord, the promise of an eternal kingdom) have been integrated into an eschatological framework. Finally the new earth and the new heaven will be very different from the old because sin will be no more.

Another good illustration of how Jews understood the kingdom of God is found in Assumption (or Testament) of Moses 10:1–10. Probably first written around 170 B.C. before the Maccabean revolt and then revised sometime between A.D. 7 and 30 (see chaps. 6—7), this rewriting of Moses' farewell speech in Deuteronomy 31—34 presents an overview of Israel's history and ends with a picture of God's kingdom in the future.[3] The author discerns a three-stage pattern in Israel's history. The apostasy that characterized Israel's life after the entrance into the land of Canaan was punished with the destruction of Jerusalem and its temple in 587 B.C., and the restoration after the Exile was at best a partial vindication. But then the cycle repeated itself. Israel's evil deeds after the restoration constituted apostasy, and the persecution unleashed under Antiochus IV Epiphanes around 170 B.C. is the punishment. This time the vindication will be complete, for it will be the coming of God's kingdom. The author believes in nonviolence and sees the martyrdom of the pious Jews as the mechanism that will trigger the coming of the kingdom.

Chap. 10:1–10 describes the happy outcome of Israel's history and its total vindication as a people:

> [1] And then His kingdom shall appear throughout all His creation,

And then Satan shall be no more,
And sorrow shall depart with him.

2 Then the hands of the angel shall be filled
Who has been appointed chief,
And he shall forthwith avenge them of their enemies.

3 For the Heavenly One will arise from His royal throne,
And He will go forth from His holy habitation
With indignation and wrath on account of His sons.

4 And the earth shall tremble: to its confines shall it be
shaken:
And the high mountains shall be made low
And the hills shall be shaken and fall.

5 And the horns of the sun shall be broken and he shall be
turned into darkness;
And the moon shall not give her light, and be turned wholly
into blood.
And the circle of the stars shall be disturbed.

6 And the sea shall retire into the abyss,
And the fountains of waters shall fail,
And the rivers shall dry up.

7 For the Most High will arise, the Eternal God alone,
And He will appear to punish the Gentiles,
And He will destroy all their idols.

8 Then thou, O Israel, shalt be happy,
And thou shalt mount upon the necks and wings of the
eagle,
And they shall be ended.

9 And God will exalt thee,
And He will cause thee to approach to the heaven of the
stars,
In the place of their habitation.

10 And thou shalt look from on high and shalt see thy enemies
in Ge(henna),
And thou shalt recognize them and rejoice,
And thou shalt give thanks and confess thy Creator.

(R. H. Charles)

The first part of the passage (vv. 1–2) reinforces points
about the kingdom already made in 1 Enoch: God as the
principal agent ("his kingdom shall appear"), the acknowledgment of God in all creation ("throughout all his creation"),
and sin's departure. It adds the notion that the coming of the
kingdom will be accompanied by a battle between the forces of

evil with Satan as leader and the forces of good with the angel "who has been appointed chief." Here the Old Testament tradition of holy war has been integrated into the framework of the last day and given cosmic dimensions. The second part (vv. 3–10) also reiterates familiar features of God's kingdom: God as the principal agent ("the Most High will arise"), the coming of God's kingdom as the vindication of righteous Israel, and the reinterpretation of old traditions. This section adds the notion that cosmic signs will accompany the coming of the kingdom: earthquakes, astral phenomena, drying up of the waters (vv. 4–6).

How did Jews in Jesus' time understand the kingdom of God? Though some guerrilla movements may have tried to force God's hand by armed uprisings, these two texts look to the time when *God* will fulfill his promises to Israel and establish his kingdom for all to acknowledge. It is a *future* kingdom. When the course of Israel's history has been played out, God will vindicate his people. The kingdom will be a *new age*. The evil ones will be punished and destroyed, and goodness and righteousness will prevail. In keeping with the major concern in this book, it is worth observing here the role that being righteous plays in being part of God's people in the future kingdom. Being an Israelite by birth is not enough to guarantee membership. One must be righteous too.[4]

JESUS' PREACHING OF THE KINGDOM

In Mark 1:15 the first saying attributed to Jesus is obviously intended to summarize his preaching: "The time is fulfilled and the kingdom of God is at hand; repent and believe in the gospel." To what extent did Jesus agree with then current views about the kingdom of God, and to what extent did he differ from them? A number of parables in the synoptic Gospels begin with the expression "the kingdom of God (or heaven) is like . . . ." The very least that these parables tell us is how the Evangelists and the early church understood the kingdom of God. But in their most primitive forms many of the parables are generally considered to be the product of the historical

Jesus, and so it is very likely that the perspectives presented in them tell us about Jesus' own understanding of the kingdom.

Analysis of some of the shorter kingdom parables reveals present and future dimensions in Jesus' teaching. Mark 4:30–32 (see Matt. 13:31–32) compares the kingdom to a mustard seed from which there grows a tree eight to ten feet high, one so large that birds come from all directions and rest in it. The chief point of the parable seems to be the contrast between the smallness of the seed and the size of what comes from it. The major emphasis is on the spectacular outcome, but the presence of the mustard seed itself implies that something is already happening now. Present and future dimensions are combined. Again in Matt. 13:33 (Luke 13:20–21) the kingdom is compared to the process of making bread. If you add only a little amount of leaven (like yeast or baking powder) to three measures of flour, you come out with enough bread to feed a hundred people. The point here too is the contrast between small beginnings in the present and the great product in the end. The comparisons of the kingdom with treasure hidden in a field (Matt. 13:44) and with the pearl of great price (Matt. 13:45–46) revolve around the value of the objects found and the total commitment demanded by them ("he went and sold all that he had"). These objects exist now, and something can be done now. The parable of the dragnet in Matt. 13:47–50 takes an experience that would have been very familiar to people who lived around the Sea of Galilee—drawing in a net full of fish and sorting out the good from the bad. That experience is used as an image of what is going to happen in the divine judgment accompanying the coming of the kingdom, a judgment in which good and bad will be separated. So Jesus' teaching about the kingdom of God is very much in line with that of his contemporaries with respect to the future. There will be a clearer and more obvious manifestation of God's kingly rule than there is at present (mustard seed, leaven, hidden treasure, pearl). Moreover that manifestation will involve a judgment in which the righteous and unrighteous will be separated (dragnet). Jesus takes for granted the hopes for the coming kingdom so characteristic of his time, but his stress on the present aspects of the kingdom sets him somewhat apart. The kingdom is present now even if only in a small way (mustard seed, leaven), but for those who perceive its presence, the kingdom demands total commitment (hidden treasure, pearl).

The present dimensions of Jesus' teaching on the kingdom are underscored by several sayings in the synoptic tradition that have a fairly good claim to be from the earthly Jesus.[5] In response to his opponents' doubts regarding the source of his power as an exorcist, Jesus says in Luke 11:20 (see Matt. 12:28): "But if it is by the finger ("spirit" in Matthew) of God that I cast out demons, then the kingdom of God has come upon you." The expression "finger of God" alludes to the signs performed by Pharaoh's magicians and Moses (Exod. 8:19). The Gospel saying explains that God is the source of Jesus' power and that the healings performed in Jesus' ministry are present experiences of the kingdom. Another saying expressing the present aspects of the kingdom is Matt. 11:12 (see Luke 16:16): "From the days of John the Baptist until now, the kingdom of heaven has suffered violence, and men of violence take it by force." The interpretation of this saying is very complex, but for our purposes the point is that the kingdom is enough of a present reality as to suffer violence and opposition. The time of God's activity as king is now. John the Baptist marks a decisive shift in history, and the present age is a time of conflict. A third significant saying about the presence of the kingdom occurs in Luke 17:21: "The kingdom of God is in the midst of you." The mystical or spiritualizing interpretation frequently read into this saying ("the kingdom is within you") is inconsistent with Jesus' view of the kingdom as something "out there" and is by no means demanded on philological grounds. Rather, Jesus seems to be rejecting the typically Jewish view that the kingdom cannot come without signs and portents (see Assumption of Moses 10). He asserts that it is already present ("among you"). These three sayings confirm the present dimension of Jesus' teaching on the kingdom. The exorcisms are present manifestations of the kingdom (Luke 11:20). From John the Baptist to Jesus, the kingdom is enough of a present reality that it can be opposed (Matt. 11:12). The kingdom is in the midst of us, and there is no need to search out signs (Luke 17:21). What precisely is this present aspect of the kingdom? These sayings and many others in the synoptic tradition imply that the present dimension is none other than the healing and teaching ministry of Jesus. In other words the kingdom of God is inaugurated in the person of Jesus himself.

Was Jesus in his insistence on the present aspect of the kingdom simply going back to the earlier Israelite concept of the kingship of Yahweh? Was he merely dismissing the future-oriented speculations of his contemporaries? A glance at the second petition in the Lord's Prayer ("thy kingdom come," Matt. 6:10; Luke 11:2) shows that no is the answer to both questions. In fact there is a group of sayings attributed to Jesus that seems to put the coming of the kingdom in the immediate future. Just before the story of the transfiguration Jesus says in Mark 9:1 (Matt. 16:28; Luke 9:27), "Truly, I say to you, there are some standing here who will not taste death before they see the kingdom of God come with power." In the so-called eschatological discourse, Mark 13:30 (see Matt. 24:34; Luke 21:32) seems to assert that the events of the "last day" will occur in this generation: "Truly, I say to you, this generation will not pass away before all these things take place." Matt. 10:23 ("Truly, I say to you, you will not have gone through all the towns of Israel before the Son of man comes") implies that the Son of man will come to exercise judgment in the eschaton before the disciples are able to cover all the area of Israel in their missionary efforts.

All three future sayings begin with "truly" ("amen"), one of the modes of speech considered by some to be characteristic of the earthly Jesus.[6] At any rate, these are not the kind of sayings that would have been created by and placed on Jesus' lips by the early church since these events did not occur nearly as soon as the sayings envision them. The conclusion that Jesus spoke about the kingdom as coming soon seems inescapable. How then are these sayings to be interpreted? In the history of exegesis they have been explained as referring to the transfiguration, the death and resurrection, Pentecost, or the destruction of Jerusalem.[7] But any interpretation that does not point to the imminent coming of the kingdom seems artificial. One can account for the sayings by asserting that Jesus was simply mistaken, or that Jesus was adapting himself to the conventions of his time, or by any formulation between these two extremes.[8] The point for our purposes is that both the present and the future dimensions of the kingdom of God were important to Jesus.

JESUS AND THE CHURCH

In the preaching of Jesus the full flowering of the kingdom of God is future. It is the work of God himself, and our efforts cannot bring it about or build it up. It will come to fullness only at the end of history as we know it, on the Day of the Lord. It will have arrived when all creation acknowledges God's reign and sin is no more. But the kingdom is also (at least in part) a present reality. The healing and teaching activities of Jesus constitute its inaugurated aspects, and its present dimensions demand a decision for or against it. Some surprising people like tax collectors and public sinners make a positive commitment to it.

Is this present or inaugurated aspect of the kingdom of God the same as the church? Not exactly! The present dimension of the kingdom resides in the person of Jesus. The church is the community of those who believe in Jesus and his preaching of the kingdom. It preserves and repeats Jesus' preaching and tries to be faithful to it. It lives its life against the background or horizon of the kingdom. As the community of Jesus Christ it is the sign and symbol of hope for the future. But the kingdom is not the same as the church. The church is the people of God here and now, the gathering of believers awaiting the coming of God's kingdom ("thy kingdom come"), embracing the righteous and those striving to be so. The church as the people of God is the fellowship of aspirants to the kingdom gathered in the name of Jesus Christ and led by the Spirit of God. It is the sign that the kingdom has been inaugurated in the person of Jesus and will come to completion whenever God wishes. It announces the kingdom, but is not the kingdom itself. The facile identification of the kingdom and the church runs the risk of deifying the church and making it more of an ultimate reality than it deserves to be. The New Testament writers were careful to avoid confusing the kingdom of God and the church as the people of God.

Granted that the church is the community of Jesus Christ, did Jesus found the church? The origins of the church lie in the entire action of God in Jesus Christ, but the decisive moment was the resurrection when the proclaimer of the kingdom became the one proclaimed. God's action of raising up the crucified one and pouring out the Spirit turned the group of disciples into the church. Hans Küng makes this point very well: "As soon as people gathered together in faith in the resurrection of the crucified Jesus of Nazareth and in expectation of the coming consummation of the reign of God and the return of the risen Christ in glory, the church came into existence."[9] When the question whether Jesus founded the church is placed in this context, the answer is that God in Jesus founded the church.

But this is not the usual context in which the question is asked. Generally when the question is raised, "Jesus" refers to the earthly Jesus in the course of his public ministry and before the passion, death, and resurrection. The term "found" has to do with establishing a consciously planned social institution, and "church" suggests a sociologically definable institution with a given structure. So when most people today ask, "Did Jesus found the church?" they really mean, "Did the earthly Jesus intend to establish an ecclesiastical organization?"[10] This question elicits widely divergent responses. Some argue that Jesus of Nazareth did found a clearly defined ecclesiastical organization and put Peter at its head as a kind of replacement for Jesus. Others maintain that the church was a mistake, a rather poor substitute for the kingdom. They cite (unfairly and inaccurately) A. Loisy's famous formula: "Jesus preached the kingdom of God, and what came was the church."[11] In my opinion, both these extreme positions overlook the elementary sociological mechanisms by which religious movements develop.

Jesus came to preach the kingdom of God, not to start an ecclesiastical organization. In Max Weber's sociological terminology, he was a charismatic prophet: "a purely individual bearer of charisma, who by virtue of his mission proclaims a religious doctrine or divine commandment."[12] Convinced of his special mission from God and seeking validation only from God, Jesus proclaimed the coming of the kingdom of God. Jesus did not rely very heavily on the existing institutional models available in Jewish society of his time. He did not found a school like the rabbis or a closed community like Qumran or an exclusivist circle like the Pharisees. His preaching and his healing activity were available to all kinds of people (even tax collectors and sinners) and seem to point logically beyond the confines of Israel. Apparently the earthly Jesus had no intention of confining his ministry within the boundaries of a neatly defined and closed organization. Furthermore, Jesus showed little concern with the privileges and structural prerogatives of his earliest disciples (e.g. Mark 10:42–45). What counts is their preaching of the kingdom, and their life-style is that of wandering preachers (e.g. Matt. 8:18–22; Luke 9:57— 10:16) and not of supervisors of local cells.[13]

In the pre-Easter period, the preaching and healing activity of Jesus did, however, furnish a basis for the emergence of the church in the postresurrection period. A group within Israel (the disciples of Jesus) had already been impressed by the content of Jesus' preaching and devoted themselves to him. By accepting the teaching of Jesus these disciples were already different from other Jews of their time. Instead of abandoning these teachings after Jesus' death, the disciples treasured and proclaimed them. Also, there was a continuity in personnel between Jesus' disciples before his death and those who bore witness to him after the resurrection. In both cases the Twelve and the women were the central characters. There were even continuities in practice. The church's common meals commemorating Jesus' death and resurrection surely had their origin in his sharing of meals with tax collectors and sinners. The church's free attitude toward the Law and the Pharisaic tradition can be traced back to Jesus' own example. Even baptism "in the name of Jesus" surely had its root in the eschatological ritual of moral purification practiced by John the Baptist. These continuities of belief, personnel, and practice between the group gathered around Jesus in his earthly ministry (the disciples) and the group gathered around the risen Lord (the church) furnished the basis for the emergence of the ecclesiastical institution that we call the church.

The emergence of the church as a sociological institution is best viewed in the light of Max Weber's idea of the "routinization" of charisma; that is, the process by which either the prophet or his disciples secure the permanence of his preaching and the congregation's distribution of grace.[14] In the instance of early Christianity the charismatic personality, teaching, and activity of Jesus formed the impulse that led to "routinization" by the early church over a fairly long period of time.

Yet there is a text that has traditionally been cited as proof that Jesus did intend to found a new religion with a fixed organizational pattern. It is the promise to Peter[15] in Matt. 16:18: "You are Peter and on this rock I will build my church." This text and Matt. 18:17 are the only instances in which the word "church" (*ekklēsia*) is placed on Jesus' lips. There is a longstanding debate over whether or not the earthly Jesus would have said "church." If "church" means a full-blown ecclesiastical institution, probably not. If it simply means "holy community," it is not at all impossible, especially in the light of similar titles having been applied to the Qumran community ("community of God"). But perhaps the debate is misplaced. On the most literal reading of the text, Jesus' promise to build a church is to come to pass in the future. It occurs in the context of a passion prediction (Matt. 16:13–23) and presumably is to be fulfilled in the time after Jesus' death and resurrection. Even here the church is primarily a post-Easter phenomenon, though Peter emerges as an important principle of continuity with the earthly Jesus.

CONCLUSION

Jesus' primary task was preaching the kingdom of God. He was a charismatic prophet, and he showed little or no interest in establishing a highly structured organization or a new religion. Jesus' beliefs and practices as well as the circle of his earliest disciples provided the preparation and furnished the continuities for the emergence of the church after the resurrection. The development of the early church should be seen as the "routinizing" of Jesus' charisma. The church is the community of aspirants to the kingdom of God gathered in the name of the risen Lord and led by the Holy Spirit. The crucial event in the founding of the church is the death and resurrection of Jesus. Through baptism Christians share in that foundational event and become members of God's people in Christ. Nevertheless, the fundamental "Jewishness" of early Christianity must not be ignored. In the formative stages of the Christian community neither Jesus nor his disciples disavowed Judaism as a religious orientation. The followers of Jesus considered themselves as a movement within Judaism and were considered such by others.

NOTES

1. H. Küng, *The Church* (London: Burns and Oates, 1967), pp. 127–30.

2. J. T. Milik, *The Books of Enoch, Aramaic Fragments of Qumrân Cave 4* (Oxford: Clarendon, 1976).

3. D. J. Harrington, "Interpreting Israel's History: The Testament of Moses as a Rewriting of Deut 31—34," in *Studies on the Testament of Moses,* ed. G. W. E. Nickelsburg, SBLSCS 4 (Missoula, Mont.: Scholars Press, 1973), pp. 59–70.

4. L. Ettmayer, "Kirche als Sammlung Israels?" *ZKT* 100 (1978): 127–39, makes a similar point about the Qumran community.

5. N. Perrin, *Rediscovering the Teaching of Jesus* (New York and Evanston: Harper & Row, Publishers, 1967), pp. 63–77.

6. J. Jeremias, *New Testament Theology: The Proclamation of Jesus,* trans. J. Bowden (New York: Charles Scribner's Sons, 1971), pp. 35–36.

7. M. Künzi, *Das Naherwartungslogion Matthäus 10,23: Geschichte seiner Auslegung,* BGBE 9 (Tübingen: Mohr-Siebeck, 1970); and idem, *Das Naherwartungslogion Markus 9,1 par: Geschichte seiner Auslegung mit einem Nachwort zur Auslegungsgeschichte von Markus 13,30 par,* BGBE 21 (Tübingen: Mohr-Siebeck, 1977).

8. Jeremias in *New Testament Theology,* pp. 139–41, views these sayings as spiritual judgments (that is, "God has granted a last period of grace; make use of the time before it is too late") and not forecasts of the date. Jesus did not dictate to the Father the precise time of the kingdom, and God is free either to shorten the time (Mark 13:20) or to lengthen it (Luke 13:6–9).

9. Küng, *The Church,* p. 109.

10. A. Cody, "The Foundation of the Church: Biblical Criticism for Ecumenical Discussion," *TS* 34 (1973): 3–18.

11. Küng, *The Church,* p. 69.

12. M. Weber, *The Sociology of Religion,* trans. E. Fischoff (Boston: Beacon Press, 1964), p. 46.

13. G. Theissen, *Sociology of Early Palestinian Christianity,* trans. J. Bowden (Philadelphia: Fortress Press, 1978).

14. Weber, *The Sociology of Religion,* pp. 60–61.

15. R. E. Brown et al., eds., *Peter in the New Testament: A Collaborative Assessment by Protestant and Roman Catholic Scholars* (Minneapolis: Augsburg Publishing House, 1973; New York, Paramus, and Toronto: Paulist Press), pp. 83–101.

CHAPTER 3

The Earliest Church as
an Apocalyptic Community

We have described Jesus' primary task as preaching the kingdom of God and defined the church as the community of aspirants to that kingdom. Since the coming kingdom of God was the dominant concept in Jewish apocalypticism, it is fair to call Jesus an apocalyptic preacher and the earliest church an apocalyptic community. What does this mean for our understanding of the church as the people of God? Rather than mining the early parts of the Acts of the Apostles for information about the first Christian community, I prefer to develop an analogy between two contemporary Jewish apocalyptic communities—the Qumran community that gave us the so-called Dead Sea scrolls and the church at Jerusalem that is at the root of the traditions presented in Acts 1—2. The primary concerns in this discussion will be the basic interests of the two communities, their distinctive theological outlooks, and their institutions and self-understandings. This comparison is intended to provide a means of penetrating the overlay of Lucan interpretation in Acts 1—2 and of enabling us to make some fairly reliable statements about the first Christian community.

THE QUMRAN SECT AS
AN APOCALYPTIC COMMUNITY

The Qumran scrolls were first discovered in 1947 by the shores of the Dead Sea, some twenty or thirty miles east of Jerusalem.[1] Dating from between 150 B.C. and A.D. 70, the scrolls include Hebrew texts of Old Testament books, Hebrew

33

and Aramaic texts of books like Jubilees and 1 Enoch, some Greek fragments, and hitherto unknown books. The Rule of the Community (or Manual of Discipline, as it is frequently called) is something like the constitutions of a religious order in which the community's ideology and practical activity are freely blended. The document has a long literary history,[2] and the best copy we have comes from the first quarter of the first century B.C. The Rule of the Community gives us a firsthand glimpse of how a group in Jesus' time holding the theology of Jewish apocalypticism saw itself and structured itself. Our task here will be to analyze a few passages from the Rule (designated 1QS) in an effort to understand the basic interests of the Qumran community (1:1–13), its apocalyptic theology (3:15–21; 4:15–19), and its structures and self-designations (8:1–10).

The first few lines of the rule (1:1–13) are part of a report concerning the rite of entrance into the community (1:1—3:12) and serve to illustrate some important points about the Qumran sect that are duplicated in many other texts. Founded some one hundred and fifty years before the birth of Jesus and still existing forty years after his death,[3] this community saw itself as the place in which the Scriptures were properly interpreted and fulfilled: "to seek God with all their heart and all their soul, and do what is good and right for him, as he commanded by the hand of Moses and his servants the prophets" (1:1–3).[4] Living in a kind of monastic solitude by the shores of the Dead Sea, the sect viewed itself as a school of perfection in which the Old Testament Law could best be fulfilled and practiced. It took up residence by the Dead Sea because the founding members were convinced that those who controlled the media of salvation in Jerusalem (the temple worship and the interpretation of the Scriptures) had gone astray. The so-called Pesharim and other documents show that a primary activity of the sect was the study of the Scriptures in an effort to understand how these were being fulfilled in the very history of the sect. The community itself became the key that could unlock the mysteries of the Scriptures. Second, the community made a clear distinction between good and evil deeds and between the people who did good and those who did evil: "to depart from all evil and cling to all good works" (1:4–5). Morality was very important for this group, and its members traced good and evil back to God by identifying good as what "he has chosen" and evil as what "he has despised." So we have a Jewish group dedicated to doing good and avoiding evil that placed these actions in the apocalyptic theological framework of the struggle between God's forces and the forces of evil. Third, this community saw itself as formed by God's grace and as the place of his covenant: "to practice the precepts of God in the covenant of grace, that they may be united in the council of God and behave perfectly before him" (1:7–8). In all Jewish piety the covenant with God is a key concept, but in this passage and elsewhere in the scrolls the concept is narrowed down to those who follow the community's inspiration and rules. The sect believed itself to have been constituted by God's grace or favor ("the covenant of grace") and as the special place of covenant keeping vis-à-vis the other forms of Judaism. Finally, this group practiced community of goods: "all the volunteers that cling to his truth shall bring all their understanding and powers and possessions into the community of God" (1:11–12). All the prospective member's spiritual and mental abilities, physical powers, and money and worldly goods were placed at the disposal of the group. Interpretation of the Scriptures, ethical dualism, the covenant of grace, and community of goods emerge in the first few lines of the rule as some of the community's basic interests.

Rule of the Community 3:13—4:26 is a fairly long discourse summarizing the sect's apocalyptic theology. Its content is much like the kingdom-of-God passages in 1 Enoch and Assumption of Moses treated in the previous chapter, but its manner of expression is more theoretical and indeed almost metaphysical. The ultimate director of history is God himself ("from the God of knowledge comes all that is and shall be," 3:15), and he has given humankind dominion over the earth ("it is he who made man that he might rule over the earth,"

3:17–18). There are also two forces or powers outside the person ("he allotted unto man two spirits") that can influence one's conduct ("that he should walk in them"). These two spirits will retain their influence in human affairs "until the time of his visitation" (3:18), that is, until the coming of God's kingdom on the Day of the Lord. The sect's apocalyptic theology is aptly described as a "modified dualism" in that God has the ultimate control over the forces of good and evil. Now there are two opposing camps. On the one side are the prince of light (an angelic figure like Michael), the sons of light (members of the Qumran sect and other good people), and the good deeds. On the other side are the prince of darkness (another angelic figure called Belial or Mastema in the Dead Sea scrolls or Satan in the New Testament), the sons of darkness (people who do evil), and the evil deeds. The pattern of modified dualism explains why there are good and evil people in the world, but all of this is coming to an end with God's visitation on the last day and the coming of his kingdom. Similar points are made toward the end of the discourse (4:15–20), but this section adds the idea that each person has both good and evil aspects "according to whether he has much or little" (4:16). If the good spirit predominates, the person belongs to the children of light; if the evil spirit predominates, the person is part of the children of darkness. The section 4:16–19 gives us information about the coming kingdom: the present time is a struggle between the spirit of good and the spirit of evil, but at the final visitation God will put an end to the spirit of perversity and establish truth forever. These passages in the instruction on the two spirits provide a more general and philosophical version of the apocalyptic theology found in 1 Enoch and Assumption of Moses that we studied in the previous chapter. Its basic points can be summarized in this way: Everything proceeds according to God's plan. The individual is viewed as an element in the cosmic struggle now going on between good and evil, and action now determines what lot one belongs in. At the final divine intervention evil will be destroyed and truth will be established forever.

The passage in Rule of the Community 8:1–10 that tells us about the community's structure and self-consciousness occurs in the part of the document (5:1—9:26) dealing with community regulations. It is especially important in calling into question two long-standing but false assumptions that haunt discussions about the earliest forms of the church: (1) As an eschatologically oriented or apocalyptic community, the early church had no interest in structures or fixed patterns. (2) Ecclesiastical offices arose only when apocalyptic fervor for the coming kingdom waned. The Qumran sect was surely convinced that the Day of the Lord would come soon and still developed clearly defined structures and procedures. Column 8 begins: "In the council of the community there shall be twelve men and three priests." These people seemed to have served as a board of directors or inner circle among the fully initiated members. The twelve men correspond to the twelve tribes of Israel descended from the twelve sons of Jacob, and the three priests correspond to the three priestly families descended from the sons of Aaron (Gershon, Kohath, and Merari). Besides the structural function of this council, there is an obvious symbolic value by which the inner circle is a microcosm of all Israel, lay and priestly. These officials are to be especially qualified and experienced in the sect's goals and ideals. Other Qumran texts speak of an overseer who tests those entering the community, judges transgressions of the Law and the community's rules, supervises business transactions, and administers the common treasury. Those entering the sect must undergo a two-year period of testing, and only then do they take their places among the fully qualified "many." The passage in Rule of the Community 8:1–10 goes on to apply to the community epithets reserved for Israel as God's elect people or for the Jerusalem temple: the house of holiness for Israel, the company of infinite holiness for Aaron, an everlasting planting, appointed to offer expiation for the earth, the tried wall, the precious cornerstone, the dwelling of infinite holiness for Aaron, the house of perfection and truth in Israel (lines 5–10). The point behind this mass of titles is that the temple in Jerusalem is in the hands of sinners but within the Qumran community the ideal of priestly holiness is practiced to such an extent that this community functions as the true spiritual temple. So the Qumran community appears from this text as a structured apocalyptic group and as applying to itself titles expressing an ideal of priestly holiness.

The Qumran community is an example of a Jewish religious movement that existed in Jesus' time and was guided by an apocalyptic theology. Study of parts of one of its important documents, Rule of the Community, reveals many obvious points of contact with the early church and serves as a very useful control for talking about the earliest Christian church according to Acts 1—2.

THE CHURCH IN ACTS 1—2

The first seven chapters of the Acts of the Apostles purport to tell the story of the earliest Christian community at Jerusalem. Luke based these chapters on traditions treasured in the Jerusalem church or some other Palestinian community, but he shaped his sources rather freely in accord with his interests and those of his community, probably around A.D. 80 (e.g. the destruction of Jerusalem, the difficulty of missionary activity, persecution from Jews and pagans).[5] Far from getting a straightforward and direct report of the early days of the church in Acts, we are given some early sources interpreted and expanded in the light of the concerns of churches some fifty years after the events being described there. One recent treatment of both the Gospel of Luke and the Acts of the Apostles argues that establishing the church's claim to be the people of God was one of Luke's major interests in editing the traditions about Jesus and the first Christians.[6] A recent analysis of the structure of Acts 1—15 suggests that the book begins with the assertion that only Jesus is the means of salvation (chaps. 1—5). This is followed by a treatment of the two traditional institutions thought by Israel to be the means of salvation: the temple and the Law. Stephen's speech in Acts 7 became an explanation for the destruction of the temple; the temple worship was no longer acceptable because Jesus had not been accepted. Then chaps. 8—14 prepare for the claim that the Mosaic law is not necessary for salvation.[7]

In talking about the earliest Christian community on the basis of Acts we necessarily see through a glass darkly, but perhaps the comparison with the Qumran community may allow us to catch a glimpse at least of that church's interests, theology, and institutions. Few, if any, scholars today see a direct or genetic relationship between the two groups. In other words, the early church is not to be explained as an outgrowth of the Essene or Qumran movement. But the comparison of these two Jewish apocalyptic communities active in the same general locale in Palestine in the second quarter of the first century A.D. might provide a way of penetrating through Luke's editorial filter and reaching the earliest church.

The very first chapter of Acts identifies the disciples gathered in Jerusalem as an apocalyptic community. Their question to the risen Lord in Acts 1:6 makes that clear: "Lord, will you at this time restore the kingdom to Israel?" They are instructed to remain in Jerusalem and await the coming of the Holy Spirit and the beginning of their mission as witnesses (1:4, 8). The picture of the disciples gathered together in prayer in the upper room (1:12–14) and their concern to replace Judas and so reconstitute the group of Twelve (1:15–26) are preparation for some dramatic event that is to occur soon. The most obvious points of contact between these Christians and the Qumran community involve waiting for the decisive intervention of God, having members gather for exercises of piety, and according to the number twelve a structural and symbolic value. But some features distinguish the Jerusalem church from the Qumran movement: its urban setting as opposed to the Qumran brand of monasticism, the sense that in Jesus the decisive events are not only imminent but also already occurring, and the prominence of mission and of sharing the good news. So Acts 1 establishes the Jerusalem church as an apocalyptic community, but not of precisely the same type as Qumran.

On Pentecost (Acts 2:1–13) the power of God (or Holy

Spirit) comes upon the assembled community and empowers them for the mission. Then in Peter's speech (Acts 2:14–36) we have Luke's formulation of the earliest apostolic preaching. In the introduction to the speech (vv. 14–21) Peter explains the events of Pentecost[8] in the light of Joel 3:1–5: "And in the last days it shall be, God declares, that I will pour out my Spirit upon all flesh . . ." The Old Testament passage speaks of the prophetic spirit of "the last days," the cosmic signs before the Day of the Lord, and salvation for those who call upon the name of the Lord. The similarities between this passage and the previously cited selections from 1 Enoch, Assumption of Moses, and Rule of the Community establish Joel 3:1–5 as a piece of eschatology. What is significant in Acts 2 is that the events of Pentecost which had already occurred are being interpreted as part of the events of "the last days." The "already" aspect of Jesus' eschatological preaching is being extended to include the coming of the Spirit upon the disciples after Jesus' death and resurrection. Then after summarizing the essential facts of Jesus' life, death, and resurrection (Acts 2: 22–24), the speech offers proofs from the Old Testament that Jesus was destined to be raised from the dead. The details of the passages need not concern us here, but the important point for our purposes is that Jesus is taken as the key that unlocks the mysteries of the Scriptures. The first text is Ps. 16:8–11, which describes a righteous sufferer whom God has delivered from death: "For thou wilt not abandon my soul to Hades, nor let thy Holy One see corruption." The exposition of the text in Acts 2:29–32 argues that David was not talking about himself but rather about his descendant Jesus who "was not abandoned to Hades, nor did his flesh see corruption." The second text is Ps. 110:1, in which God speaks to the newly crowned king of Israel and tells him to sit at his right hand: "The Lord said to my Lord, sit at my right hand, till I make thy enemies a stool for thy feet." The exposition (vv. 33–36) assumes that David could not have been talking about himself because he did not ascend to the heavens and so he must have been talking about his descendant Jesus who had been exalted to the heavens.

The selections from the Psalms are cited here to demonstrate that Jesus fulfills the promises of the Old Testament and that the Old Testament confirms Jesus.

So both the Jerusalem church and the Qumran community focused on the Day of the Lord and the events accompanying it. Moreover, both communities were convinced that the Old Testament Scriptures were being fulfilled in the present and within their group. The primary and most obvious difference between the two communities is Jesus Christ. The death and resurrection of Jesus changed everything for the early church. According to Acts 2 the death and resurrection of Jesus had already initiated the sequence of eschatological events. According to Acts 2 the Scriptures are fulfilled in Jesus, not in the community as at Qumran. The inaugurated eschatology and the notion of Christ as the key to the Scriptures set the earliest church as it is glimpsed in Acts apart from the Dead Sea sect.

At the end of Peter's discourse in Acts 2 there are some important indications about the institutions of the Christian community. In v. 38 Peter says, "be baptized every one of you in the name of Jesus Christ for the forgiveness of your sins." The term *baptize* means "to dip down or immerse in water," and the Qumran community had a very elaborate system of ritual washings and a keen interest in ritual purification. But the baptism practiced by John the Baptist provides a better analogue for Christian baptism than the Qumran ritual washings. John's baptism occurred once rather than repeatedly, emphasized moral purity rather than ritual purity, and prepared the person for the Day of the Lord. The early Christians, however, gave this baptism a specifically christological orientation ("in the name of Jesus Christ"). Christian baptism was not only a sealing for the eschaton but also the symbolic appropriation of the present salvation proclaimed by Jesus.[9] In Acts 2:42 the Christians are described as devoting themselves "to the apostles' teaching and fellowship, to the breaking of bread and prayers." Our concern here is the breaking of bread. The term *breaking of bread* comes from the initial action of the Jewish meal in which bread was blessed, broken, and distributed. The Qumran community celebrated common meals and understood them as anticipations of the messianic banquet to take place on the last day (see 1QS 6:2–5; 1QSa 2:17–22). A similar rationale existed for the Christian communal meal, but its distinctive feature again is its direct connection to Jesus. The meal is a remembrance of Jesus and points toward the eschaton (see Luke 22:15–20). Finally the earliest church is said in Acts 2:44–45 to have practiced community of goods: "And all who believed were together and had all things in common; and they sold their possessions and goods and distributed them to all, as any had need." Those entering the Qumran community surrendered their possessions to the common fund much as those entering religious orders do. The early Christians practiced a different form of community of goods (see Acts 4:32—5:11). Whenever there was need for money for the poor within the church, one of the property-owning members would sell some valuables or a piece of property and present it for distribution by the church leaders. Both the Qumran movement and the Jerusalem church practiced ritual purification, had common meals, and shared goods. Once more the decisive difference between the two groups revolves around the person of Jesus.

At the beginning of this section we drew attention to the difficulties encountered in gathering information about the earliest Christian community in Jerusalem. But even though Acts 1—2 shows many traces of Luke's editorial hand, the analogy with the Qumran movement helps us glimpse some features of the Jerusalem church. It seems safe to say that this first Christian community awaited the intervention of God, gathered for exercises of piety, saw the number twelve as significant, viewed Christ as the key to the Scriptures, practiced baptism, held meals in common, and shared its goods.

CONCLUSION

Although there is no evidence of a direct relationship between the Qumran sect and the earliest Christian community in Jerusalem, the Dead Sea scrolls provide a firsthand glance at a Jewish eschatological community contemporary with the Jerusalem church. Faith in the death and resurrection of Jesus as God's decisive intervention in human history sets the church apart from the Qumran sect. Many of the specific features distinguishing the two groups become much clearer when we turn to the earliest written documents preserved in the New Testament—Paul's letters.

NOTES

1. For a recent review of research, see G. Vermes, *The Dead Sea Scrolls: Qumran in Perspective* (Cleveland: William Collins & World Publishing Co., 1978).

2. J. Murphy-O'Connor, "La genèse littéraire de la *Règle de la Communauté*," *RB* 76 (1969): 528–49. See also J. Pouilly, *La Règle de la Communauté de Qumrân: Son évolution littéraire,* Cahiers de la Revue Biblique 17 (Paris: Gabalda, 1976).

3. J. Murphy-O'Connor, "The Essenes in Palestine," *BA* 40 (1977): 100–124.

4. The English translations are adapted from A. Dupont-Sommer, *The Essene Writings from Qumran,* trans. G. Vermes (Cleveland and New York: World Publishing Co., 1962).

5. R. J. Karris, *Invitation to Acts* (Garden City, N.Y.: Doubleday & Co., Image Books, 1978). For details, see E. Haenchen, *The Acts of the Apostles: A Commentary* (Oxford: Basil Blackwell, 1971).

6. G. Lohfink, *Die Sammlung Israels: Eine Untersuchung zur lukanischen Ekklesiologie,* SANT 39 (Munich: Kösel, 1975).

7. J. J. Kilgallen, "Acts: Literary and Theological Turning Points," *BTB* 7 (1977): 177–80.

8. For the theological significance of Pentecost in Jewish belief, see J. Potin, *La fête juive de la Pentecôte: Étude des textes liturgiques,* LD 65 (Paris: Cerf, 1971).

9. G. Lohfink, "Der Ursprung der urchristlichen Taufe," *TQ* 156 (1976): 35–54.

CHAPTER 4

Baptism into Christ

(*Galatians 3*)

One of the most famous and frequently quoted texts in the New Testament is Gal. 3:28: "There is neither Jew nor Greek, there is neither slave nor free, there is neither male nor female; for you are all one in Christ Jesus." A consensus has emerged that the verse was originally a pre-Pauline baptismal formula.[1] According to this formula, baptismal incorporation into Christ has rendered racial, social, and sexual distinctions ultimately unimportant. The passage is usually cited today in the debate about the role of women in the church. But emphasis on the phrase "neither male nor female" seems to have distracted us from what for Paul was the far more important part of the formula—"neither Jew nor Greek." If we read Paul's Letter to the Galatians against the background of his conflict with Christians under the spell of a Judaizing form of Christianity, then we see that the real point of the passage in which the formula appears and indeed of the whole letter comes in 3:29: "And if you are Christ's, then you are Abraham's offspring, heirs according to promise."[2]

Gal. 3:6–29 is especially significant for our understanding of the church as the people of God. First, it makes perfectly clear how we (whether we be Jew or Greek) become a people—in and through Christ. Second, it wrestles with the all-important relation between the people of the old covenant and the people of the new covenant in Christ. This part of our study will explore (*a*) the situation in which Paul wrote the Letter to the Galatians, the place of 3:6–29 in the plan of the epistle, the

45

basic point of the passage, (*b*) the use made of biblical texts in the course of the argument, and (*c*) the role of the Law in God's plan of salvation.

THE TEXT

Paul wrote this letter in the mid-fifties to the Christian community in Galatia, an area in Asia Minor to which he had brought Christianity. While Paul continued on with his missionary activities, people in Galatia were becoming infatuated with a different, more traditionally Jewish variety of Christianity. The major objection to Paul's gospel involved the terms on which the Gentiles like the Galatians were to be accepted into the church. Should they be circumcised and take upon themselves the other obligations incumbent upon observant Jews? The Judaizing opponents say yes, and Paul replies with a decisive no. It is important to have clearly in mind the identity of Paul's opponents in this letter. They are not simply Jews. Rather they are Jews or Gentiles who confess Jesus of Nazareth as the Messiah but still maintain that Gentiles must "go through" Judaism in order to become genuine Christians.[3] To them Christianity remained securely within the confines of Judaism. If Gentiles wish to be part of God's people in Christ, they must be circumcised and do what observant Jews do. This brand of Christianity, and not simply Judaism in general, is the object of Paul's arguments in the Epistle to the Galatians.

After the customary epistolary introduction (1:1–5) and the expression of amazement at what is going on among the Galatians due to the troublemakers (1:6–9), Paul presents a personal and historical defense of his gospel (1:10—2:21) as revealed by the Lord, as approved by the chief apostles, and as the only valid gospel. In 3:1—4:31 Paul argues his case by appealing to the Old Testament to demonstrate that Christians are the heirs to the promises made to Abraham and that Gentile Christians share in these promises by faith and not by circumcision and observance of the Law. Finally Paul warns the Galatians not to lose their freedom in Christ because of circumcision (5:1–12), to act in accordance with the "law of Christ" (5:13—6:10), and to live in Christ as "the Israel of God" (6:11–18). At stake in the Letter to the Galatians is the validity of Paul's mission to the Gentiles and the whole theology of how sinful people can find right relationship with God. It is both a personal letter that gives insight into Paul's character and a controversial letter that measures his gospel against that of the Jewish-Christian opponents.

What does the structure of the Letter to the Galatians mean for the interpretation of 3:6–29? The passage is part of a document in which the central issue is how Gentile Christians can be part of "the Israel of God." The opponents in the debate are Jews by race who have accepted Christ but maintain that Gentiles must become Jews first in order to be genuine Christians. The issue is, Who has the true gospel for the Gentiles, Paul or his opponents? Paul's answer is that his is the true gospel because baptism into Christ is sufficient to make one part of God's people and an heir to the promises made to Abraham. Circumcision and strict observance of the Law are unnecessary, and so Gentiles do not have to take upon themselves all the specific obligations incumbent upon observant Jews in their efforts to remain part of the Israel of God.

Galatians 3:6–29 is a tour de force in which Paul demonstrates that he can outdo his opponents at their own game of biblical interpretation. They claim to base their case on Scripture. Well, Paul wants to show that his case too rests upon Scripture. They claim that their position is the only one consistent with the divine revelation in the Law. Well, Paul wants to show how his position is even more consistent with the biblical revelation. But the complexity of Paul's argument should not be allowed to obscure his three basic points. First, people of faith are the children of Abraham, and conversely Abraham is the model of Christian faith: "So you see that it is men of faith who are the sons of Abraham" (v. 7). Second, what allows the Gentiles to become Abraham's offspring and part of God's people is baptism into Christ: "For as many of you as were baptized into Christ have put on Christ" (v. 27). Third, Christ makes it possible for the Gentiles to be part of the promises made to Abraham: "If you are Christ's, then you are Abraham's offspring, heirs according to promise" (v. 29).

These points are made at the beginning and end of an extremely difficult passage. Furthermore, they have become so familiar that their dimensions can pass us by. Perhaps we can grasp what Paul says by making clear what he does not and does say. He does not say that belonging to the people of Abraham is unimportant or meaningless. He does say that belonging to the people of Abraham is essential to right relationship with God. He does not say that circumcision and observance of the Mosaic Law are the means of becoming children of Abraham. He does say that one becomes part of this tradition by way of incorporation into Christ through baptism. He does not say that Christ began a totally new religion. He does say that one becomes part of the Jewish tradition by taking Abraham as the model of faith. In a sense Abraham is the "first Christian."[4] Relation to Israel of old, baptism into Christ, faith after the pattern of Abraham—these are the essential features in Paul's understanding of the church as the people of God.

THE SCRIPTURES

Between the beginning and the end of his argument Paul tries to establish his case by interpreting the Scriptures and by explaining the function of the Law. The very establishing of his case brings out some of the problems connected with the use of "people of God" as a title applied to the church.

Taking Gen. 15:6 as the starting point of the scriptural argument, Paul says that Abraham "believed God, and it was reckoned to him as righteousness." The pattern of justification by faith illustrated in the case of Abraham is said to apply to all people of faith so that they constitute the children of Abraham (vv. 6–7). To confirm this point, he weaves a web of biblical quotations and personal comments. In v. 8 he cites

Gen. 12:3 (or 18:18) to the effect that all the nations are blessed in Abraham, and adds in v. 9 that faith is the means by which this blessing is appropriated. Then he uses Deut. 27:26 to argue that those who rely on the works of the Law are under a curse (v. 10), Hab. 2:4 to show that one is justified by faith (v. 11), Lev. 18:5 to demonstrate that faith and the Law are antithetical principles (v. 12), and Deut. 21:23 to affirm that Christ redeemed us from the curse of the Law (v. 13). All of these texts are marshaled in the service of Paul's basic argument expressed in v. 14: "that in Christ Jesus the blessing of Abraham might come upon the Gentiles, that we might receive the promise of the Spirit through faith."

If we were to trace each of these quotations back to their biblical contexts and interpret them according to the principles of modern biblical scholarship, we would probably soon become confused and disappointed. In order to understand what Paul is doing, we must try to grasp and respect the historical conditions of his exegesis. In his argument with the Jewish Christian opponents, the "proof from Scripture" would have special significance. Moreover, the Scriptures were viewed by Paul and his contemporaries as a divine mystery or riddle that must be solved by recourse to some principle of interpretation. Whereas the Qumran community found the key to the Scriptures in the history and the life of their own group, Paul and other early Christian interpreters found Jesus Christ to be the key that unlocks the mystery of the Scriptures. Paul's basic hermeneutical principle is that the Old Testament Scriptures were talking about Christ.

Christ is the key to the Scriptures. This fundamental principle of interpretation allowed Paul to discover Christian meanings even in the words of the Old Testament. For example, in the Old Testament *faith* means fidelity or loyalty to Yahweh, but in Gal. 3:6–14 and elsewhere in the Pauline corpus faith also involves the appropriation of the Christ-event and its effects. Faith is faith in the promise of Christ, and even Abraham can be viewed as the prototype of Christian faith. Likewise, in the Old Testament "all the nations" (v. 8) refers to the

political entities surrounding and threatening Israel (Egypt,
Assyria, Edom). But to Paul and his contemporaries the term
has a more religious connotation. It means "the Gentiles,"
those non-Jewish individuals who had now become part of
God's people in and through Christ. Finally, the Law in the
Old Testament is first and foremost divine instruction, the
revelation of God's will for Israel, the plan for God's people.
Paul, however, seizes upon a misuse of the Law. He criticizes
the Law as a principle by which people try to justify themselves and work out their salvation apart from God. This
attitude misuses the Law and turns it into a means of attempting to control or manipulate God. So we see that Paul takes
up several biblical quotations and interprets them according
to a grid of Christian equivalencies: "faith" is Christian faith,
"the nations" are individual Gentiles, and "the Law" is the
principle of self-justification. He does this in the light of his
fundamental principle of biblical interpretation: Jesus Christ
is the means of solving the mysteries of God's revelation. This
point is made quite clearly in 2 Cor. 3:14–16 when Paul
contrasts the reading of the Old Testament by non-Christian
Jews with the Christian reading: "But their minds were hardened; for to this day, when they read the old covenant, that
same veil remains unlifted, because only through Christ is it
taken away. Yes, to this day whenever Moses is read a veil lies
over their minds; but when a man turns to the Lord the veil
is removed."

THE LAW

This framework of biblical exegesis allows us to understand the use of "to his offspring," from Gen. 12:7, and other
texts in Gal. 3:15–18. The Genesis texts speak of the promises
having been made to Abraham and "his seed" or offspring.
The most natural way of understanding the Hebrew word for
"seed" is to take it as a collective noun referring to the many
descendants of Abraham. Paul takes another road. He seizes
on the fact that "seed" is singular in form and insists that it
must refer to one person and that this person is Jesus Christ:

" 'And to your offspring,' which is Christ" (v. 16). Then he plays with the ambiguity of the Greek term *diathēkē* ("covenant" and "will" or "testament") to introduce his discussion regarding the relation between the promise or covenant given to Abraham and the Law. Just as no one annuls or makes additions to a will that has been ratified, so the Law which according to the biblical chronology came four hundred thirty years after the promise to Abraham cannot be viewed as an annulment of or an addition to that promise.

Why then the Law? If the mysteries of the Old Testament are resolved in Christ and if Christ gives access to the promises made to Abraham and so to right relationship with God, what was the function of the Law in the divine plan? As we have seen, in genuine Jewish piety the Torah is God's way for his people and is to be taken very seriously. Paul sees Law-oriented piety as a negative force, but that does not absolve him from attempting a description of its positive significance. The fact that Paul gives several reasons, and even these are not fully developed, suggests that the busy missionary had not thought through the matter as lucidly as we would like. It is essential to keep in mind that Paul is dealing with a pressing pastoral problem: Do the Gentiles need to be circumcised and undertake the obligations of the Law to become real Christians?

Paul's first effort at explaining the role of the Law in salvation history comes in vv. 19–20: "It was added because of transgressions, till the offspring should come." What is clear in these verses is that according to Paul the Law is secondary ("it was added") and provisional ("till the offspring [Christ] should come"). He then cites a Jewish tradition (see Bk. Jub. 1:27; 2:1, 26–27; Acts 7:37–38, 53) that the Law was "ordained by angels through an intermediary" and uses it to suggest that the Law was inferior to the promise made to Abraham. The phrase "because of transgressions" is not entirely clear but seems to mean that the Law specifies crimes or even tempts one to sin. The second explanation (vv. 21–22) involves the idea that through the Law "the Scripture consigned all things to sin." In other words, the Law was designed to reveal the absolute necessity of the Christ-event as the way of justification and so was not contrary to the promise given to Abraham. By making us conscious of the all-pervasive character of sin, the Law had the effect of showing us that faith is the principle of justification and one becomes part of Abraham's people through faith. The third explanation (vv. 23–25) views the Law as "our custodian until Christ came." The Greek word for custodian is *paidagōgos*—the origin of our English term *pedagogue*. But the *paidagōgos* was not the teacher. Rather he was a slave charged with leading the master's child to and from school and with supervising his conduct while the child was still a minor. The point of the metaphor is that while we were still immature we needed the Law but now (in Christ) we have reached maturity and no longer need our custodian.

What then is the place of the Law in God's plan? According to Paul the Law was secondary to the promise made to Abraham, provisional until Christ's coming, and inferior to the promise. Furthermore, the Law revealed the absolute necessity of grace and the Christ-event as the only effective means of bringing about right relationship with God. Finally, it served as a guardian while we were young and needed supervision. As the conclusion to his reflection on the functions of the Law, Paul says, "in Christ Jesus you are all sons of God through faith" (v. 26). Unlike the Law, Christ forms us into a people of God and the principle of appropriating this status is faith—a faith patterned after the example of Abraham.

ABRAHAM IN ROMANS 4

Before recapitulating the contributions of Gal. 3:6–29 to our understanding of the church as God's people in Christ, we might glance at Paul's portrayal of Abraham in Rom. 4:1–25.[5] Its place in the overall structure of the epistle will be clear from the discussion of Romans at the beginning of the next chapter. Here we are only concerned with the confirmation that it supplies to Paul's thesis that Christians are the real children of Abraham. In Rom. 4:1–25 Paul proposes three arguments taken from the example of Abraham. First, Abraham was justified by faith (vv. 1–8). Beginning once more from Gen. 15:6 ("Abraham believed God, and it was reckoned to him as righteousness"), Paul presents Abraham's submission to the divine promise that he would have a son (and through him great offspring) as revealing the structure of genuine faith. Second, Abraham was reckoned as righteous before God prior to his circumcision (vv. 9–12). According to the biblical chronological scheme, the promise of offspring to Abraham and his response of faith (Gen. 15:1–6) took place twenty-nine years before circumcision was introduced as the sign of the covenant (Gen. 17:9–14). Therefore circumcision was the sign or seal of the covenant with Abraham, and not the vehicle of his justification. Abraham is the father of the uncircumcised and circumcised alike, and circumcision without the faith of Abraham goes for naught. Third, the promise to Abraham is fulfilled only for the believer who acts according to the model of Abraham (vv. 13–25). Whereas in authentic Judaism the Law is seen as the vehicle of the promise and the two cannot be separated, Paul sets them in an antithetical relationship and insists that the promise to Abraham is not bound to the Law. Sharing the faith of Abraham is what counts toward right relationship with God (v. 16). The God whom Abraham believed is the God of resurrection faith, the one who raised up Jesus (v. 24) and "gives life to the dead" (v. 17). In Abraham's first encounter with God in Gen. 12:1–3 he was told to go to the land that God would show him and where he would become the father of a great nation. The problem was that Abraham had no children from his wife Sarah. So on the one hand Abraham had the divine promise that he would be the father of a great nation, and on the other hand he had the grim realities of his own old age and his wife's sterility. In this situation "no distrust made him waver concerning the promise of God, but he grew strong in his faith as he gave glory to God, fully convinced that God was able to do what he had promised" (vv. 20–21). Far from being simply an admirable character out of ancient history, Abraham furnishes the pattern for faith here and now ("not for his sake alone but for us also"). Thus in Rom. 4:1–25 Paul argues that Abraham was justified by his faith in God's promise, not by circumcision, which was at most the sign or seal of the covenant. Abraham emerges as the model for "us who believe in him that raised from the dead Jesus our Lord" (v. 24).[6] The example of Abraham allows Paul to develop an idea that he had raised in his warning to the Philippians concerning those who insisted that Christians be circumcised: "For we are the true circumcision, who worship God in spirit, and glory in Christ Jesus, and put no confidence in the flesh" (Phil. 3:3).

CONCLUSION

In Gal. 3:6–29 Paul insists that belonging to Christ makes one part of the people of God and heir to the promises made to Abraham: "If you are Christ's, then you are Abraham's offspring, heirs according to promise" (v. 29). Faced with Jewish-Christian preachers who maintained that the Gentiles had to be circumcised in order to be genuine Christians, Paul maintained that incorporation into Christ in baptism, and not circumcision and observance of the Law, allows the believer to be part of "the Israel of God" (6:16). What emerges from the debate is the absolute centrality of Christ in forming the people of God. Christ makes it possible for Gentiles to be children of Abraham. Christ is the key that unlocks the mysteries of the Scriptures. Christ does what the Law could not do; he brings about right relationship with God. The church's claim to be God's people is based solely on Christ.

NOTES

1. W. A. Meeks, "The Image of the Androgyne: Some Uses of a Symbol in Earliest Christianity," *HR* 13 (1974): 165–208.

2. H.-F. Weiss, " 'Volk Gottes' und 'Leib Christi': Überlegungen zur paulinischen Ekklesiologie," *TLZ* 102 (1977): 411–20.

3. K. Stendahl, *Paul Among Jews and Gentiles and Other Essays* (Philadelphia: Fortress Press, 1976). See also W. D. Davies, "Paul and the People of Israel," *NTS* 24 (1977): 4–39.

4. E. Käsemann, "The Faith of Abraham in Romans 4," in *Perspectives on Paul,* trans. M. Kohl (Philadelphia: Fortress Press, 1971), pp. 79–101.

5. E. Käsemann, *An die Römer,* HNT 8a (Tübingen: Mohr-Siebeck, 1973), pp. 98–121.

6. Compare T. Lorenzen, "Faith without Works Does Not Count before God! James 2:14–26," *ExpTim* 89 (1978): 231–35.

CHAPTER 5

The People of God
in Romans 9–11

Paul had not founded the church at Rome and had not even visited Rome before he wrote his Letter to the Romans in the middle or late fifties of the first century A.D. The large Jewish population at Rome was the context in which Christianity arose and developed and became a significant force by the forties of the first century A.D. There were also Gentile Christians in the Roman community, and the difference between the Jewish and the Gentile Christians became particularly prominent with the expulsion of the Jews from Rome in A.D. 49. When the Jews (and of course the Jewish Christians) were allowed to return in A.D. 54, the tensions between Jews and Gentiles within the Christian community became serious.[1] After all, presumably the Gentiles had the church all to themselves during the absence of the Jewish Christians. So in writing to the Romans Paul was again dealing with a pressing pastoral problem—the relationships of the Gentile Christians to the Jewish Christians at Rome, to the Jewish heritage of Christianity in general, and to those Jews (by far the majority) who had not accepted Christ.

In addition to furnishing advice to the Christians at Rome, Paul probably had another good reason for writing this letter. He wanted to make Rome the base of his mission in the west and from there move on to Spain (see 15:24, 28). Remaining faithful to his apostolic principle of not building on another's foundation (see 15:20), Paul wished to visit Rome and then push on toward the west. But before he could put these plans into operation, he had to wind up the business of the collection for the church in Jerusalem (see 15:25). That trip to Jerusalem was not going to be a simple business transaction of delivering the proceeds of the collection to the church officials there. Besides being a concrete way of expressing the unity of the various Christian communities with the Jerusalem church, Paul's presentation of the gifts was probably to be a time for explanations regarding his conduct of the Gentile mission.[2] In other words, Paul foresaw that he was going to have to explain his pastoral practice once more (see Gal. 2:1–10; Acts 15:1–35), and so he took the Letter to the Romans as an occasion for articulating a defense of his gospel of justification apart from the observance of the Jewish Law.

So the Epistle to the Romans, which is ostensibly the most theological and most systematic of the Pauline letters, arose as a response to two pastoral situations. On the one hand, Paul was anxious to shed light on and reach some kind of resolution regarding the problems between the Gentile Christians and the Jewish Christians at Rome. On the other hand, he wished to explain how he could preach a gospel apart from observance of the Law. The major problem in the background was the status of Gentile Christians with respect to the Jewish Christians and to Israel: How could these Gentiles be part of the people of God without taking upon themselves the obligations that characterize true Israelites?

The major concern in this chapter is the complex of relationships between groups as they are spelled out in Romans 9—11. Among the most complicated passages in the Bible, this text twists and turns through a difficult argument that Paul the pastoral theologian may not have worked through completely at every point. These chapters are part of a long meditation concerning the revelation of God's righteousness to all who have faith (Rom. 1:16–17).[3] After demonstrating the need for the revelation of God's righteousness (1:18—3:20), Paul shows that we are justified by grace on God's side and faith on our side after the pattern of Abraham (3:21—4:25). Then he establishes the nature of Christian freedom as

liberation from death, sin, and the Law and for life in the
Spirit (5:1—8:39). Chaps. 9—11 deal with the plan of God
and the place of Israel in it, while 12:1—15:13 explores the
ramifications of God's righteousness in everyday life. The
remainder of the epistle is concerned with Paul's travel plans
(15:14–33) and personal greetings (16:1–27). In this outline chaps. 9—11 constitute one of the real focuses of the
argument. Far from being an appendix or an afterthought,
these chapters are the goal for which Paul had been preparing
in the first eight chapters. Now he must directly address why
there are Gentiles in the church, why not all Israel had accepted the gospel of Jesus Christ, and what the future holds
for the church and for the Jewish people.

How is Romans 9—11 significant for our understanding of
the church as the people of God? Too frequently the use of
the title seems to involve a simple and straightforward transfer
of Israel's prerogatives to the church. But that kind of "replacement" thinking masks a number of serious problems that
only Paul among the New Testament writers has treated in
any depth. These are the questions that Paul courageously
faces in Romans 9—11: By what right does the church composed of Jews and Gentiles take to itself the privileges of
Israel? How can Gentiles be considered part of God's people?
Has God rejected Israel as his people and so been unfaithful
to his promises? What is the significance of the Gentile acceptance of the gospel and the Jewish rejection of it? Will all
Israel finally be saved? The difficulty of the passage demands
that we pay careful attention to the course of Paul's argument.

THE CHURCH AS THE PRESENT GOAL OF
SALVATION HISTORY (9:1–29)

In the introduction (9:1–5) to the passage Paul expresses
sorrow that not all Israel has turned to Christ but acknowledges the great privileges granted to and retained by Israel.
The legal language of v. 1 ("I am speaking the truth . . . I
am not lying . . . my conscience bears me witness") yields
to the language of human emotion in vv. 2–3. So great is

Paul's attachment to his fellow Jews that if it would do any good, he would be accursed and cut off from Christ for their sake. Israel's historic privileges as God's people are listed and affirmed. To them belong sonship (see Exod. 4:22), the glory (that is, the presence of God), the covenants (with the patriarchs), the Law, the worship (that is, the temple cult), the promises, the patriarchs, and Christ himself. Then in the first major section of his argument (9:6–29) Paul seeks to establish that the recipient of God's promise is the church rather than Israel according to the flesh (vv. 6–13), that the direction of salvation history depends entirely on God's will (vv. 14–23), and that the church made up of Jews and Gentiles is the present (though provisional) goal of that salvation history (vv. 24–29).

Paul firmly believes that the promises and privileges of Israel have reached their fulfillment in Christ, but the fact that not all Israel agrees casts doubt upon the efficacy of God's word. Paul must demonstrate that the word of God has not failed. First in vv. 6b–8 he contests the view that physical origin determines one's status in the history of salvation. According to him, the children of Abraham are those who believe that the promise to Abraham has been realized in Christ ("the children of the promise"). Then in vv. 9–13 he shows by appeal to the children born of Sarah and Rebecca that God always has and still does deal with people on the basis of promise or call, not on the basis of flesh or works. In other words, Israel cannot use its claim of physical descent from Abraham to argue that the church composed of Jews and Gentiles is not God's people. The bearer of the divine promise to Abraham is the church, not Israel according to the flesh.

Is God unfair? To answer this objection Paul sets up a "chosen-rejected" pattern of Old Testament figures. Isaac was chosen but Ishmael was rejected (v. 10). Jacob was chosen but Esau was rejected (vv. 12–13). Moses was chosen but Pharaoh was rejected (vv. 15, 17). Because God is God, the direction of history depends upon his will: "So it depends not upon man's will or exertion, but upon God's mercy" (v. 16).

Is God unfair? In Paul's perspective we have no more right to ask this question of God than a lump of clay molded into a piece of pottery has the right to question the potter (vv. 20–23). God's plan cannot be measured by human criteria.

Finally in vv. 24–29 Paul asserts that the present, though provisional, goal of salvation history is the church composed of Jews and Gentiles: "even us whom he has called, not from the Jews only but also from the Gentiles" (v. 24). Using Hos. 2:23 (see 1 Pet. 2:10) to prove his point, he insists that the "not my people" and the "not my beloved" (that is, the Gentiles) have become "my people" and "my beloved." Then citing Isa. 10:22–23, he seeks an explanation for Israel's unbelief in the idea of the remnant: "only a remnant of them will be saved" (v. 27).

Up to this point Paul has established the church as the bearer of the divine promise, the sovereignty of God in directing salvation history, and the church made up of Jews and Gentiles as God's people and as God's beloved.

UNBELIEVING ISRAEL (9:30—10:21)

In the second part of his reflection on the relationship between the church and those Jews who have not accepted Christ, Paul seeks for explanations. Why do so many of his fellow Jews still not see Jesus as the culmination of Israel's religious heritage? The first line of explanation (9:30–33) concerns the use made of the Law. Paul claims that these unbelieving Israelites committed the fundamental error of thinking that the works of the Law could insure their right relationship with God. The Gentiles who did not pursue right relationship with God have attained it through faith after the pattern of Abraham. Thus they deserved to be part of God's people. But those Israelites who so vigorously pursued right relationship with God have failed to attain it. Why? Because they put all their energies into the Law and failed to recognize Jesus as the promised Messiah. This Jesus now constitutes the stumbling block for such Jews (9:33; see Isa. 28:16; 8:14; 1 Pet. 2:6–7).

The second line of explanation (10:1–4) revolves around
Christ as "the end" of the Law. After expressing his fondest
wish that all Israelites be saved and after criticizing their zeal
as not enlightened (vv. 1–2), Paul defines the nature of the
unbelieving Israel's guilt: they did not understand that righteousness comes from God, and they tried to establish their own
brand of righteousness and did not submit to God's way of
righteousness. When Paul calls Christ the "end" of the Law,
he uses the (probably deliberately) ambiguous term *telos* to
make his point. Is Christ the finish of the Law or the goal of
the Law? He would be "the finish" of the Law if he rather than
the Law were seen as a legitimate principle of bringing about
right relationship with God. Then Christ would be replacing
the Law. But that is not the only way Paul views Christ and
the Law. Rather, the real thrust or goal of the Law according
to Paul was to prepare for and show the necessity of Christ's
coming and the consequent unification of all peoples.[4] The
unbelieving Israelites should have recognized that Christ is
both the finish and the goal of the Law.

The third line of explanation (10:5–13) is that acceptance
of the Christian gospel rather than observance of the Law is
the way of salvation. Paul begins by contrasting Lev. 18:5
("the man who practices the righteousness which is based on
the Law") with Deut. 30:11–14 and connects the near word
of the covenant mentioned in the text of Deuteronomy with
the Christian gospel ("the word is near you"). Then in vv.
9–11 he takes up the Deuteronomy text to make the point that
belief and confession of that belief lead to justification and
ultimately to salvation. God is the lord of all, and everyone
who calls on his name—whether Jew or Greek—will be saved.

Why do some Israelites remain unbelieving? They wrongly
think that the works of the Law can bring about justification.
They fail to recognize Christ as "the end" of the Law. They
reject the proclamation of the good news about Christ. The
gospel has been preached (vv. 14–15), but not all Israel has
heeded the gospel (v. 16). Vv. 18–20 rob these Israelites of
any ground for pardon. Have they not heard? Ps. 19(18):4

is used to establish the preaching of the gospel in every place. Have they not understood? The combination of Deut. 32:21 and Isa. 65:1 is seen as referring to the preaching of the gospel to the Gentiles and their acceptance of it. Israel should have understood that the Gentile acceptance of the gospel was a significant sign. Instead it has rejected God's near word— the gospel.

THE PRESENT AND THE FUTURE (11:1–36)

In chap. 11 Paul makes a courageous effort to think through systematically the mystery of salvation history. First in vv. 1–10 he establishes that Israel's obduracy is not total. The fact that he himself—an Israelite, a descendant of Abraham, a Benjaminite—has accepted Christ means that God has not rejected his people entirely (vv. 1–2a). Just as in Elijah's time there was a remnant in Israel, so in the present time the Jewish Christians like Paul constitute "a remnant, chosen by grace" (v. 5). The Jewish-Christian remnant as the elect has obtained what Israel sought, but a kind of hardening has come upon those Jews who have not accepted Christ (vv. 7–10).

Having described the present significance of the Jewish Christians with respect to the unbelieving part of Israel, Paul now turns in vv. 11–24 to the relation between the Gentile Christians and the unbelieving part of Israel. Paul proposes the daring idea that the inclusion of the Gentiles will make unbelieving Israel so jealous that it too will accept the gospel. He sees the present stumbling of Israel as the God-given opportunity to make available to the Gentiles the blessings reserved for God's chosen people (vv. 11–12). Apparently Paul feels obligated to remind the Gentile Christians at Rome of their spiritual roots in Judaism. If the Jewish rejection of the gospel has meant the reconciliation of the Gentiles (and the world they represent) to God, then the Jewish acceptance of the gospel will mean "life from the dead" (v. 15). Paul may be hinting here that the ultimate reconciliation of Israel will take place on "the Day of the Lord"—in the eschatological display of God's power when the dead are restored to life.[5] That would suggest that the salvation of "all Israel" in v. 26 is an eschatological event to occur when all creation acknowledges God as the Father of Jesus Christ. But at this point in his argument Paul is still primarily interested in the present. God's plan of salvation is compared to an olive tree in vv. 17–24. The root of the tree remains the people chosen by God from of old. Those Jews who have not accepted Christ are viewed as branches broken off from the olive tree, and those Gentiles who have accepted the gospel are seen as shoots grafted onto the olive tree. Notice that Paul does not conceive the church as made up only of Gentiles. Notice also that for Paul there is no salvation for the Gentiles apart from the people of Israel. In vv. 19–22 Paul insists that membership in God's people is not an occasion for pride or self-congratulation, and he urges the Gentiles to look with awe at the working out of God's plan. Moreover, he is confident that God will graft those broken branches (the unbelieving Israelites) back into the olive tree (the people of God) just as he is now grafting shoots from the wild olive tree (the Gentile Christians) onto the cultivated olive tree (Israel). The qualification made in v. 23 regarding the reinsertion of the broken branches ("if they do not persist in their unbelief") seems to speak against this being a strictly eschatological event affected by God alone (see v. 15). It appears to suggest that the way of reinclusion is through the faithful appropriation of the gospel, in the here and now, not in the eschatological action of God.

Finally in vv. 25–27 Paul outlines for us his vision of God's saving plan: "a hardening has come upon part of Israel, until the full number of the Gentiles come in, and so all Israel will be saved." The mystery that Paul discerns involves the inclusion of the Gentiles into the people of God, the present hardening of part of Israel, and the future salvation of all Israel. Whether this future salvation of Israel is purely eschatological ("what will their acceptance mean but life from the dead?" in v. 15) or begins now ("if they do not persist in their unbelief" in v. 23) is not entirely clear. What is clear is that the gifts and the call of God are irrevocable (v. 29), and this means that in the end God will certainly have mercy on his people. For all his efforts at discerning and specifying God's plan in history, Paul remains a humble but enthusiastic admirer of it: "O the depth of the riches and wisdom and knowledge of God! How unsearchable are his judgments and how inscrutable his ways!"

Thus in chap. 11 Paul has argued that the acceptance of the gospel by Jewish Christians like himself means that Israel's obduracy has not been total. Furthermore he has discerned a threefold process being worked out by God: the present hardening of part of Israel, the inclusion of the Gentiles, and the final salvation of all Israel.

CONCLUSION

In the light of this exposition of Romans 9–11 we can see the outlines of Paul's answers to the questions confronting him. (1) By what right does the church composed of Jews and Gentiles take to itself the privileges of Israel? It does so because of its belief that the promises made to Abraham reach their fulfillment in Christ and that Christians accepting Christ in faith are the real children of Abraham. (2) How can Gentiles be considered part of God's people? The Old Testament itself speaks of a "not my people" and a "not my beloved" becoming part of God's people, and these passages are cited to show that the inclusion of the Gentiles is part of God's plan. (3) Has God rejected his people and so been unfaithful to his promises? God has certainly not rejected Israel. Some Israelites like Paul have accepted the near word of the gospel, though a large part of Israel has rejected it. At any rate, for Paul a church without any relationship to Israel is unthinkable. (4) What is the significance of the Gentile acceptance of the gospel and the Jewish rejection of it? The partial Jewish rejection of it has inspired the possibility of preaching the gospel to the Gentiles, and the Gentile acceptance of it will make unbelieving Israel jealous enough eventually to accept the gospel. (5) Will all Israel finally be saved? Everything is proceeding according to God's plan of a partial hardening of Israel, the inclusion of the full number of Gentiles, and the salvation of all Israel. It is difficult to decide whether Paul envisioned the salvation of all Israel as due to God's eschatological intervention or to the individual acceptance of Christ prior to the eschaton. In either case the fact of the salvation of all Israel seems to be assured according to Paul.

Romans 9—11, despite all its complexity and its obscurity, reveals what a courageous thinker Paul was. These are difficult questions, and Paul did not shrink from attempting to answer them. His responses may be judged by some as inadequate or underdeveloped, yet they remain the most serious effort to grapple with these problems in the entire New Testament. In our own effort to work out the modern relationship between Christians and Jews, this passage remains a very important witness.

NOTES

1. A. Suhl, "Der konkrete Anlass des Römerbriefes," *Kairos* 13 (1971): 119–30. See now K. P. Donfried, ed., *The Romans Debate* (Minneapolis: Augsburg Publishing House, 1977); L. De Lorenzi, ed., *Die Israelfrage nach Röm 9–11*, Monographische Reihe von "Benedictina," Biblisch-ökumenische Abteilung 3 (Rome: St. Paul's Abbey, 1977); and C. L. Porter, "A New Paradigm for Reading Romans: Dialogue Between Christians and Jews," *Encounter* 39 (1978): 257–72.

2. J. Jervell, "Der Brief nach Jerusalem. Über Veranlassung und Adresse des Römerbriefes," *ST* 25 (1971): 61–73. See also K. F. Nickle, *The Collection: A Study in Paul's Strategy*, SBT 48 (Naperville, Ill.: Alec R. Allenson, 1966).

3. E. Käsemann, *An die Römer*, HNT 8a (Tübingen: Mohr-Siebeck, 1973), pp. V–VI.

4. G. E. Howard, "Christ the End of the Law: The Meaning of Romans 10:4 ff.," *JBL* 88 (1969): 331–37. See also G. S. Sloyan, *Is Christ the End of the Law?* Biblical Perspectives on Current Issues (Philadelphia: Westminster Press, 1978). Both Howard and Sloyan argue for the "goal" interpretation.

5. F. Mussner, " 'Ganz Israel wird gerettet werden' (Röm 11, 26): Versuch einer Auslegung," *Kairos* 18 (1976): 241–55. See, however, E. P. Sanders, "Paul's Attitude toward the Jewish People," *USQR* 33 (1978): 175–87, especially 178–83. See also his *Paul and Palestinian Judaism: A Comparison of Patterns of Religion* (Philadelphia: Fortress Press, 1977).

CHAPTER 6

Developments after Paul

When Paul used the term *ekklēsia* ("church"), he was referring to churches in specific places, that is, the church at Corinth or the church at Rome or the church at Jerusalem. Yet there are dimensions to Paul's theology and practice that point in the direction of a bond between local communities and of a certain kind of universalism. A universalistic outlook shaped Paul's theology. He shared the Jewish belief that the God of Israel is the God of all the universe and that there are no other gods. The need for salvation applies to Gentiles (Rom. 1:18–32) and Jews (2:1—3:20): "All have sinned and fall short of the glory of God" (Rom. 3:23). Furthermore, as the new Adam (Rom. 5) and the lord of the whole created order (Phil. 2:9–11) Jesus has worldwide significance. The church is the totality of those redeemed in Christ and believing in God's power. A universalistic or ecumenical outlook is also evident in Paul's missionary practice. Convinced that non-Jews could share in the blessings of the Christ-event, the apostle took as his special mission the preaching of the gospel to the Gentiles. He preached to Jews and Gentiles without distinction in places where the gospel had never been heard. He taught that in Christ ethnic, social, and sexual distinctions had lost their importance (Gal. 3:28). He kept in touch with various communities by sending personal emissaries and by writing letters to the local churches. By insisting that a collection be taken up for the church at Jerusalem (1 Cor. 16:1–4; 2 Cor. 8—9; Rom. 15:

25–27), he indicated that Christians of one locale are responsible for the welfare of those who live elsewhere.

Both Paul's theological outlook and his pastoral practice point beyond the local communities as being the whole story about the church. The Letter to the Ephesians and 1 Timothy (one of the so-called pastoral Epistles) seem to have been written by disciples or admirers of Paul after his death, and they develop some aspects of Pauline theology and practice in ways that were appropriate for the situations in which their late-first-century readers found themselves. In Ephesians the people of God takes on the cosmic dimensions of the body of Christ, while in 1 Timothy the line of demarcation between God's people and other peoples becomes clearer.

PEOPLE OF GOD AND BODY OF CHRIST IN EPHESIANS

The Letter to the Ephesians appears at first sight to be a letter from Paul written while he was in prison, but most modern scholars view it as an essay composed around A.D. 90 by a Jewish-Christian admirer of Paul for Gentile Christians as a means of encouraging unity within the mixed community. The literary style and the theological outlook (especially the portrayal of the church in cosmic terms) are different from that of the major Pauline Epistles. The absence of the words "in Ephesus" in 1:1 from several important Greek manuscripts has led to the theory that it was originally a general letter sent to several churches.[1] It has even been taken as an introductory essay to an early collection of Pauline Epistles. The vagueness of its language has resulted in contradictory interpretations of its background. Some see it as almost Gnostic in orientation, while others view it as an important contribution to the phenomenon of early Catholicism.[2] The first half of the letter (chaps. 1—3) celebrates the reconciliation of Jews and Gentiles in Christ, and the second half (chaps. 4—6) draws out the implications of this reconciliation for everyday Christian life.

The passage that is most significant for our discussion of the church as the people of God comes in Eph. 2:11–18, for it shows how the people made up of Jews and Gentiles forms the body of Christ. A common Christian pattern for describing the difference that accepting Christ can mean in the life of the individual believer involves the terms "once . . . but now."[3] The way of life prior to becoming a Christian is placed in stark contrast to life in the present time. But in this passage the pattern usually applied to individual conversion is being employed on a grand scale to describe the state of humanity (Jews and Gentiles) before Christ and the new state of humanity brought about through Christ.

The first part of the passage (vv. 11–12) addresses the Gentile readership of the letter but also speaks in passing about those who are Jews by birth:

> [11] Therefore remember that at one time you Gentiles in the flesh, called the uncircumcision by what is called the circumcision, which is made in the flesh by hands—[12] remember that you were at that time separated from Christ, alienated from the commonwealth of Israel, and strangers to the covenants of promise, having no hope and without God in the world.

The talk about the privileges of Israel in v. 12 is reminiscent of Paul's list of privileges in Rom. 9:4–5 (sonship, glory, covenants, Law, worship, promises, patriarchs, Christ) and emphasizes the importance of a relationship to Israel. It is impossible for Paul and for the author of Ephesians to conceive of the people of God without a connection to Israel. In order to describe the situation existing before Christ ("at one time"), the author refers to what had become a distinctive feature of Judaism in the Hellenistic world—circumcision. The Gentiles are called "the uncircumcision," and the Jews are termed "the circumcision." Once the Gentiles addressed in this letter were separated from Christ and from the promises and privileges of Israel. They had no hope and were "without God in the world." Israel's God is the only true God, and apart from the people of Israel access to God was difficult and practically impossible. Before Christ the Gentiles were separated from him.

The second part of the passage (vv. 13–18) explores how

the death of Jesus ("the blood of Christ") has made possible the unity of Jews and Gentiles into a new people close to God.

> ¹³ But now in Christ Jesus you who once were far off have been brought near in the blood of Christ. ¹⁴ For he is our peace, who has made us both one, and has broken down the dividing wall of hostility, ¹⁵ by abolishing in his flesh the law of commandments and ordinances, that he might create in himself one new man in place of the two, so making peace, ¹⁶ and might reconcile us both to God in one body through the cross, thereby bringing the hostility to an end. ¹⁷ And he came and preached peace to you who were far off and peace to those who were near; ¹⁸ for through him we both have access in one Spirit to the Father.

Again the Gentile Christians are being addressed; they "who once were far off" have been brought near to God in Christ Jesus. Christ has made Gentiles and Jews both one, has broken down the ethnic hostility that existed between the two groups ("neither Jew nor Greek"), and has abolished the Law ("Christ is the end of the Law"). V. 15b with its expression "one new man" picks up Paul's Adam-Christ typology according to which Jesus is now viewed as the new representative human being and as forming the new humanity. In v. 16 ("reconcile us both to God in one body through the cross") the reference is both to the crucified body of Christ through which reconciliation with God has been made possible and to the church as Christ's body and the place of Christ's power. According to Ephesians, the body of Christ makes Gentiles and Jews into the people of God ("one new man"). Through Christ those who were far off (Gentiles) and those who were near (Jews) have access to the Holy Spirit. Eph. 2:13–18 insists that the present unity of Gentiles and Jews has been made possible through Christ from whom there came the one new man, the one body, and the one Spirit.

Eph. 2:11–18 joins together the images of the body of Christ and the people of God. Indeed, it maintains that because of the body of Christ there is a new people of God. This collocation of images raises three important questions that must now occupy our attention: What does it mean to call the church the body of Christ? How are the various images or models of the church related? How does Eph. 2:11–18 compare with Romans 9—11?

First, the church as the body of Christ.[4] Paul compares the Christian community to a body in several passages in 1 Corinthians. In 6:15–17 he discourages sexual immorality by showing the inappropriateness of a member of the body of Christ joining himself to a prostitute: "Shall I therefore take the members of Christ and make them members of a prostitute? Never!" In 10:16–17 the eucharistic body of Christ is related to the community: "Because there is one bread, we who are many are one body, for we all partake of the one bread." The section 12:12–30 is part of Paul's attempt to deal with abuses that had come about in the meetings of the Christian community. He reminds the Corinthians that the body of Christ has many members, that all are necessary, and that Christ is the ultimate source of charismatic powers of the church. The author of Ephesians (see also Col. 1:18, 24; 2:19) develops this analogy of the church as the body of Christ by distinguishing between Christ as the head and the church as the body and by exploring the cosmic dimensions of the body. Eph. 1:22b–23 connects the lordship of Christ over all creation with the church: "and has made him the head over all things for the church, which is his body, the fullness of him who fills all in all." Whereas Paul does not draw the head-body distinction, the author of Ephesians places great emphasis on it. In the cosmic reign of Christ the church as the body of Christ has a central place, and Christ's power fills the church. This text makes a place for the church in the general plan of salvation, for the church is the place par excellence in which Christ's present reign over all creation is actualized. Eph. 4:11–16 follows 1 Cor. 12:12–30 in rooting the charisms operative within the community in the body of Christ and urges Christians "to grow up in every way into him who is the head, into Christ" (v. 15). Taking the Pauline notions of the church as the body of Christ and of the charisms in the service of the community, the author of Ephesians speaks in terms of the community's growth to maturity in Christ as head of the body. Finally, Eph. 5:21–33 expands what Col. 3:18–19 says about the mutual obligations of husbands and wives and grounds these obligations in the marriagelike relationship existing between Christ and the church. Once again Christ is the head of his body the church (v. 23), and we are members of his body (v. 30). But the passage adds the notion that the relationship between Christ and his church is so extraordinarily close that it can be portrayed in terms of a marriage. The church is the object of Christ's love: "Christ loved the church and gave himself up for her" (v. 25). Christ initiates what transpires in baptism (vv. 26–27). Marital unity reflects the unity that binds together Christ and his church (v. 32). These "body" passages in Ephesians provide the context for understanding the passage that is most central to our theme: ". . . reconcile us both to God in one body through the cross" (2:16). The body of Christ has made possible the union of Gentiles and Jews into a new people.

Second, the relations between the various images. It has become popular recently to talk about models of the church,[5] and sometimes people understand these models as opposing or contrasting principles. It is important to grasp the nature of images like "body of Christ" and "people of God." These are human attempts to describe what must finally and necessarily elude human language and human understanding—the mystery of God's relationship to humanity in Christ. A glance at New Testament Christology may help us here. The biblical writers apply a variety of titles to Jesus; for example, Son of man, Son of God, Lord, Savior, Messiah. No one of these exhausts the person of Christ, and no one of these expresses everything that there is to say about Christ. The New Testament images of the church function in much the same way. They are complementary efforts to express the various facets of the church's splendor. The New Testament authors tell us this very same thing by the way in which they use the images for the church. Just after his meditation on the people of God in Romans 9–11, Paul exhorts the Romans to act according to their understanding of themselves as the body of Christ (Romans 12:1–8). No text illustrates the point better than Ephesians 2. Our analysis of 2:13–18 has revealed that incorporation into Christ's body makes Gentiles and Jews the people of God. As the author continues in vv. 19–22, more images of the church are used:

> 19 So then you are no longer strangers and sojourners, but you are fellow citizens with the saints and members of the household of God, 20 built upon the foundation of the apostles and prophets, Christ Jesus himself being the chief cornerstone, 21 in whom the whole structure is joined together and grows into a holy temple in the Lord; 22 in whom you also are built into it for a dwelling place of God in the Spirit.

Here the Christian community is described as the city of God, the household of God, the holy temple, and the dwelling place of God. These images are piled up on top of the images of the people of God and the body of Christ. Far from opposing one another, the images not only exist side by side but even penetrate one another to the point that in v. 21 the building with Christ as the cornerstone is said to grow. So the combination of the people of God and the body of Christ in Eph. 2:16, far from being exceptional, illustrates how the images of the church can be used to illumine one another. We become the new people of God because of the body of Christ. Once again Christ is viewed as shaping the believers into a people.

Third, a brief comparison with Romans 9—11. Eph. 2:11–18 deals with some of the problems discussed by Paul in that text: How can Gentiles ("not my people") become children of Abraham and God's people? The basic answer in the two epistles is the same: in Christ. But Paul was acutely interested in Israel's present unbelief and believed that in the end all Israel will be saved. The author of Ephesians ignores the future of "unbelieving" Israel and is concerned only with the present state of the church composed of Gentiles and Jews. As for the future, the author looks only toward the "one new man" constituted by Christ. No effort is made to think out the mystery of salvation history on the same scale as Paul had done. Whether the author considered the matter resolved or no longer significant is hard to know.

These brief discussions of the church as the body of Christ, the relations between the various images of the church, and the train of thought in Romans 9—11 as compared with that in Eph. 2:11–18 digress from our central theme—the Christian community as God's people in Christ. For our purposes the most significant point in the Letter to the Ephesians is that the people made up of Jews and Gentiles forms the body of Christ. Through Christ both those who were far from God (Gentiles) and those who traditionally were near to him (Jews) have been formed into a single people. This fact is celebrated as the great mystery of God's grace in Eph. 3:6: "how the Gentiles are fellow heirs, members of the same body, and partakers of the promise in Christ Jesus through the gospel." The English translation may obscure how vigorously the author of Ephesians insisted on the theme of the one people of God. Each of the key terms in Eph. 3:6 is introduced by the Greek prefix *syn*, which means "together with" or "co-": coheirs, comembers, and copartakers. The idea of togetherness in Christ could hardly be emphasized more strongly.

THE CHURCH AND "THE OTHERS" IN 1 TIMOTHY

The reverse side of the togetherness in Christ so emphasized in the Letter to the Ephesians is the emerging tendency to distinguish the new people of God in Christ from those Jews and Gentiles who are not in Christ. At this point Christianity begins to be viewed as a new religion (though one still rooted in Judaism) and begins to display a critical attitude toward its religious opponents and society in general. The following chapter will treat three New Testament writings (1 Peter, Hebrews, and Revelation) that invoke ancient Israel's sense of peoplehood as a way of expressing the self-consciousness of the Christian community vis-à-vis Jewish and Gentile society. But a preliminary glance at the First Letter to Timothy, even though that document is not explicitly concerned with the theme of God's people in Christ, may make us sensitive to some of the sociological and theological mechanisms that served to divide Christianity from Judaism, paganism, and even forms of Christianity judged to be aberrant. These mechanisms included drawing a sharp line between truth and false teaching, relying on exemplary behavior to win others to the truth of Christian faith, putting forward the church as the household of God, and insisting on the importance of church officials.

1 Timothy along with 2 Timothy and Titus have been called the pastoral Epistles since the eighteenth century because they are addressed to Timothy and Titus as the "chief pastors" at Ephesus and Crete respectively and because they are largely concerned with their pastoral duties. The influence of these letters has been enormous in determining the outlook and the structures of the church throughout the ages. Those who defend their Pauline authorship emphasize the wealth of "personal" details and claim that they were written between A.D. 63 and 67 after Paul's release from house arrest at Rome and shortly before his death. Those who doubt Pauline authorship see the letters as composed by an admirer of Paul toward the end of the first century. The many peculiar words or words not found in other Pauline Epistles, the use of common words in un-Pauline ways, and a somewhat flat and monotonous style constitute the linguistic argument against Pauline authorship. The theological stance of the pastorals differs from the undoubtedly Pauline Epistles (Romans, 1 Corinthians, 2 Corinthians, Galatians, Philippians, 1 Thessalonians, Philemon) on several points: "faith" as a body of truth, the sharp line between orthodoxy and heresy, church offices as a safeguard of doctrine, concern for secular respectability, and little emphasis on the cross of Christ or the Holy Spirit. I see the pastorals in their present form as having been composed not by Paul but by an admirer in his name toward the end of the first century.[6] They offer advice on dealing with certain "false" teachers causing trouble in Asia Minor. They are especially significant as witnesses to some of the ways in which the church as the people of God defined itself over against its religious opponents and with respect to society in general. Several passages in 1 Timothy illustrate these strategies: the sharp line drawn between "true" and "false" doctrines (1:3–11), the adjustments made toward

the state and toward cultural standards (2:1–13), the church
as the household of God and pillar of truth (3:14–16), and
the absorption of the charisms by church officials (4:14–16).
The coming of the kingdom was not expected in the very near
future, and the people of God must make its way in the world
at large, as "a people of his own who are zealous for good
deeds" (Titus 2:14).

After the customary epistolary introduction in 1 Tim. 1:1–2,
"Paul" gives advice on true and false doctrines (vv. 3–11).
The opponents seem to have been promoting a Jewish-Christian
form of gnosis that fused elements of legalism and asceticism
grounded in Old Testament injunctions with some rather wild
speculations about the universe and salvation. They are said
to "occupy themselves with myths and endless genealogies
which promote speculations" (1:4). The description of them as
"desiring to be teachers of the law" (1:7) appears to confirm
their identity as Jews of some sort. Their prohibitions of
marriage and of certain foods mentioned in 4:3 seem to have
been rooted in a denial of the goodness of creation (4:4–5). As
a defense against the threat posed by these Jewish-Christian-
Gnostic teachers, the writer of 1 Timothy presents the Christian
ideal as "love that issues from a pure heart and a good conscience and sincere faith" (v. 5). In vv. 8–10 he takes up the
Pauline teaching about the function of the Law (see Gal.
3:19–22) as making us conscious of sin and convicting evildoers of sin. Sound doctrine and the deposit of faith (vv. 10–
11) constitute the best defense against the Jewish-Christian
Gnostics. In this passage and elsewhere in the pastorals there
is a clear division between false teaching (myths, speculations,
vain discussion) and true teaching (apostolic teaching, sound
doctrine, deposit of faith).

The second chapter of the epistle deals with public worship
and the conduct appropriate to it. The emphasis is on order
and good appearances and reflects the adaptation of Christianity
to certain social realities in the Roman world. In vv. 1–7 the
author urges that prayers be said "for kings and all who are
in high positions" in the hope that Christians may lead a peace-

able life (v. 2). Here he takes up the Pauline teaching that the state at its best can make the practice of religion easier (see Rom. 13:1–7; also compare 1 Pet. 2:13–17 and Rev. 13). Furthermore, the goal of such prayers is that all might be saved and come to the knowledge of the truth (2:4; see also 4:10). Vv. 8–13 takes up the demeanor of women in the assembly in what today seems to be a classic statement of male chauvinism. Modesty, silence, and salvation through childbearing are recommended. Situating these recommendations about women in their historical context may make them more intelligible at least. The opponents seem to have forbidden marriage (1 Tim. 4:3), and so the emphasis on childbearing is healthy. There are also indications that women were prominent in supporting the heterodox movement (see 2 Tim. 3:6). Confronted with a difficult situation in which the role of women was a major factor, the author fell back on the rigid application of generally accepted cultural norms for the status of women: subordination to men and an emphasis on the significance of childbearing. This passage taken as a whole witnesses to a willingness to view Christianity as an element within world history by cooperating with the state and by adopting general cultural standards. The Christian ideal is a quiet and peaceable life (v. 2), marked by good deeds (vv. 10, 15) and directed at winning all people to the knowledge of the truth (v. 4).

Chap. 3 describes the qualifications for bishops (vv. 1–7) and deacons (vv. 8–13) and then in v. 15 provides a theological basis for the many regulations found in the letter: "how one ought to behave in the household of God, which is the church of the living God, the pillar and bulwark of the truth." The context suggests that "household of God" is not exactly the image of the community as the temple of God as in Eph. 2:21. Rather the uses of the term "household" (*oikos*) in 1 Tim. 3:4, 5, 12 indicate that what is meant is the people who inhabit the house; that is, the family (nuclear and extended).[7] But the church, which is the family of God, is also called the pillar and bulwark of truth. These descriptions develop the "edifice" side of the *oikos* image by portraying the church as a column holding up the truth and as a firm foundation for the truth (see 2 Tim. 2:19–21). The truth that the church preserves and proclaims is summarized with the hymnic fragment cited in v. 16: "He was manifested in the flesh, vindicated in the Spirit; seen by angels, preached among the nations; believed on in the world, taken up in glory."

The final element in the author's attempt to define the church's place within the world involves the church officers. After supplying information about the opponents (4:1–5), encouraging Timothy (4:6–10), and describing Timothy's duties (4:11–13), he encourages him with these words: "Do not neglect the gift you have, which was given you by prophetic utterance when the elders laid their hands upon you" (v. 14). The Greek term for "gift" here is *charisma,* the same word that Paul used to describe the gifts of the Holy Spirit operative within the Christian community in 1 Corinthians 12 and Rom. 12:1–8. The phrase "given by prophetic utterance" envisions a public ratification of some sort, presumably in a liturgical assembly. The "presbyterate" or "elders" refers to either the older members of the community or its board of directors, and the imposition of their hands functions either as an invocation of God's blessing or as a transmission of power. The point is that the gift of the ministry of the word (see 4:11–13) is being tied to the imposition of hands by the group of elders. A similar passage occurs in 2 Tim. 1:6: "rekindle the gift of God that is within you through the laying on of my hands." The ministry of the word[8] is on its way to becoming an officially ratified position whose major function is to preserve the deposit of faith and to ensure sound doctrine.

CONCLUSION

This chapter began by looking at the universalistic dimensions of Paul's theology and missionary practice. Then the Letter to the Ephesians was seen as developing these universalistic dimensions by passing beyond concern with only the local communities and by showing how Gentiles and Jews become part of the church as the cosmic body of Christ. The new people of

God in Christ was explained in terms of the body imagery of the earlier Pauline Letters. The author of 1 Timothy responded to the threat posed by "false" teaching and the delay of Christ's second coming by insisting on a sharp division between sound doctrine and heterodoxy, external respectability with respect to the state and cultural standards, the church as the household of God and the pillar and bulwark of truth, and the church officers as safeguarding the deposit of faith. These perspectives provided the church with very effective means of defining itself with respect to the world around it and so ensured the survival of the church as the people of God.[9]

NOTES

1. B. M. Metzger, *A Textual Commentary on the Greek New Testament* (London and New York: United Bible Societies, 1971), p. 601.

2. N. A. Dahl, "Interpreting Ephesians: Then and Now," *TD* 25 (1977): 305–15; *CurTM* 5 (1978): 133–43.

3. P. Tachau, *"Einst" und "Jetzt" in Neuen Testament*, FRLANT 105 (Göttingen: Vandenhoeck & Ruprecht, 1972).

4. L. Ramaroson, "L'Église, corps du Christ, dans les écrits pauliniens: simples esquisses," *ScEs* 30 (1978): 129–41.

5. A. Dulles, *Models of the Church* (Garden City, N.Y.: Doubleday & Co., 1973).

6. B. M. Metzger, "Literary Forgeries and Canonical Pseudepigrapha," *JBL* 91 (1972): 3–24.

7. R. Schnackenburg, *The Church in the New Testament*, trans. W. J. O'Hara (New York: Seabury Press, 1965), pp. 95–98.

8. D. J. Harrington, "New Testament Perspectives on the Ministry of the Word," *Chicago Studies* 13 (1974): 65–76.

9. I am deliberately avoiding the term "early Catholicism." See my articles "Ernst Käsemann's Understanding of the Church in the New Testament," *HeyJ* 12 (1971): 246–57, 367–78; and "The 'Early Catholic' Writings of the New Testament: The Church Adjusting to World-History," in *The Word in the World: Essays in Honor of Frederick L. Moriarty, S.J.*, ed. R. J. Clifford and G. W. MacRae (Cambridge, Mass.: Weston College Press, 1973): 97–113.

CHAPTER 7

The Church as a
Minority Group

The development of the Christian communities in Asia Minor (modern Turkey) and elsewhere was hardly an untroubled march of triumph. As an apparently insignificant religious minority professing what seemed to be a new variety of Judaism, these Christians quickly found themselves at odds with devotees of pagan cults that were well established in the Mediterranean world. As a Jewish messianic movement proclaiming the coming kingdom of God, they must have attracted the suspicions of government officials seeking to preserve the political status quo. The three New Testament documents treated in this chapter—1 Peter, Hebrews, and Revelation—show how Christians who thought of themselves as "strangers and aliens" vis-à-vis the world around them drew upon imagery expressing ancient Israel's sense of peoplehood in order to express their own consciousness as a community. They call themselves God's own people (1 Pet. 2:9), learn from Israel's fruitless wanderings in the wilderness to seek heavenly rest with God (Heb. 4:9), and view themselves as priests of God and Christ (Rev. 1:6; 5:10; 20:6).

1 PETER

The clearest New Testament identification of the Christian community as God's own people occurs in 1 Pet. 2:9–10:

> 9 But you are a chosen race, a royal priesthood, a holy nation, God's own people, that you may declare the wonderful deeds

81

of him who called you out of darkness into his marvelous
light. ¹⁰ Once you were no people but now you are God's people; once you had not received mercy but now you have received mercy.

The passage begins in v. 9 by addressing the various Christians
making up the community as a chosen "race" (*genos*). The
relationship between people of various ethnic backgrounds is
so close that they can be called a "race" just as Jews by birth
could be described as a race. The next three epithets ("a royal
priesthood, a holy nation, God's own people") allude to Exod.
19:5–6, a famous passage introducing the "book of the
covenant" (chaps. 19—24). After escaping from Egypt and
wandering in the wilderness for a time, the people of Israel
encamps before Mount Sinai. Moses is told by God to warn
the people: "Now therefore, if you will obey my voice and
keep my covenant, you shall be my own possession among all
peoples; for all the earth is mine, and you shall be to me a
kingdom of priests and a holy nation" (19:5–6). The covenantal stipulations follow in chaps. 20—23. So 1 Pet. 2:9
applies to the church the designations of Israel in Exod. 19:5–6
as a priesthood dedicated to the service of God as its king, as
a nation separated from other peoples, and as a people pos-
sessed by God. Then two well-known New Testament patterns
for describing conversion (from darkness to light; once . . .
now) are used in a communal sense to describe the community's
transition from having been "no people" to being "God's people." The thrust of 1 Pet. 2:9–10 is that the new people formed
by Christ inherits the titles of ancient Israel and is bound in
such a close spiritual unity that the terms of race, priesthood,
nation, and people are entirely appropriate.

By what right does the author of 1 Peter affect this transfer
of prerogatives? Is this a simple "replacement" of Israel by
the church or has something more complicated taken place?
That "something more complicated" is the role of baptism into
Christ as creating the true children of Abraham and God's own
people. First Peter is so full of allusions to baptism that it has
frequently been interpreted as a baptismal homily or baptismal

catechesis. The immediate context of 1 Pet. 2:9–10 is the exhortation in 1:3—2:10 in which Christians are urged to live in the holiness that befits their status as the baptized. The exhortation begins with a blessing in which God is praised for his benefactions to humanity: "By his great mercy we have been born anew to a living hope through the resurrection of Jesus Christ from the dead" (1:3). Then the community is addressed: "You have been born anew, not of perishable seed but of imperishable through the living and abiding word of God" (1:23). They are urged "like newborn babes" to "long for the pure spiritual milk that by it you may grow up to salvation" (2:2). What allows the application of Israel's titles to the Christian community is faith in Christ the living stone (see Ps. 118:22) and incorporation into Christ in baptism. Once again Christ is portrayed as creating the people of God out of those baptized in his name. The train of thought is remarkably like that of Galatians 3: If we are Christ's, then we are Abraham's offspring and heirs according to promise.

What kind of community was being addressed in 1 Pet. 2:9–10? Few modern interpreters consider the document to be the composition of Simon Peter the apostle.[1] There are many affinities with the Pauline corpus, but little agreement on how to interpret them. Some see it as a deutero-Pauline letter, while others trace the affinities to the common stock of early Christian tradition. There is even some talk of a "Petrine circle." Its date of composition is not at all clear, and any time between A.D. 70 and 90 is possible. Attempts to tie it in with a specific Roman persecution have not been successful. The address given in 1:1 may help us gain an entry into the historical setting of the document: "To the exiles of the Dispersion in Pontus, Galatia, Cappadocia, Asia, and Bithynia." The recipients are addressed in the way that Jews living outside of Palestine ("the exiles of the Dispersion") would be addressed (see also James 1:1). But the emphasis on the startling change effected by baptism (see 1:14, 18; 4:3–4) and the phrase "once you were no people" in 2:10 (compare Rom. 9:25–26) indicate that Gentiles constituted a large part, if not practically the whole, of the community. The sequence of geographical sites may well reflect the route of the messenger who carried the letter in Asia Minor.[2] So the letter seems intended for a largely Gentile-Christian community in Asia Minor, a group urged to view itself as "a chosen race, a royal priesthood, a holy nation, God's own people"—all terms originally applied to Israel as God's people.

We can be even more precise about the community's situation. The passage 1:1–12 sets the tone for the whole document by describing these Christians in Asia Minor as the elect of God (v. 2) who reside only temporarily in this world.[3] They are promised the imperishable inheritance of salvation (vv. 4–5), and their present sufferings are an occasion for testing the seriousness of their faith (vv. 6–9) and their identification with Christ (vv. 10–12). The present is their "time of exile" (1:17) in which they are to conduct themselves in accord with their status as baptized Christians (1:13—2:10). These Christians are a minority group experiencing opposition from people outside the group. They are exhorted as "aliens and exiles" (2:11) to exhibit good conduct toward their pagan neighbors in the hope of giving the outsiders no reason for their opposition and perhaps even attracting them to Christianity: "so that . . . they may see your good deeds and glorify God on the day of visitation" (2:12). They are urged to avoid even the least suspicion that the church is a subversive organization and to be loyal to the governmental authorities (2:13–17). As in Rom. 13:1–7, this minority community in Asia Minor had no possibility of exerting political power or changing the system. Servants (2:18–25) and spouses (3:1–7) are advised to set a good example for pagans through their obedience and are reminded that their baptism was "an appeal to God for a clear conscience, through the resurrection of Jesus Christ" (3:21). Indeed from 3:13 onward the basic theme of the epistle is advice for those Christians who are undergoing persecution. For instance, in 4:1–6 the example of Christ is viewed as providing encouragement and sustenance in persecution: "Since therefore Christ suffered in the flesh, arm yourselves with the same thought" (v. 1). The Christians are to reflect their baptismal status in their behavior and are not to do "what the Gentiles like to do." The religious separation brought about by baptism is reinforced by a moral separation: Christians do not do what non-Christians do.

The church of 1 Peter is a distinct minority group undergoing persecution.[4] Though outsiders may view them as unnecessary and offensive, they consider themselves as the elect people of God, as heir to the traditional titles of Israel, and as playing an important role in the history of salvation. They style themselves as strangers and aliens in this world (2:11; see also 1:1, 17), but they are still involved in the society around them and hope that their good example will attract others to God.[5] The example of Christ makes their sufferings in the present time plausible and even tolerable, and their baptismal union with Christ forbids their sliding back into pagan ways.

HEBREWS

The Epistle to the Hebrews has little or nothing to do with Paul and was ascribed to him at some stages in the tradition presumably on the basis of the vague epistolary conclusion in 13:19, 22–25. Its literary style and ideas are very different from what is found in Paul's letters. In fact, Hebrews is more a discourse or a sermon than a letter. There is an unresolved controversy about the audience and date of the document, with some (especially German-speaking) scholars arguing that it was written for Gentile Christians after A.D. 70 and many other scholars maintaining that it was composed for Jewish Christians before A.D. 70. Perhaps it is better simply to say that the audience consisted of Christians outside of Palestine for whom the characters and institutions of the Old Testament were very significant.[6]

The author's primary concern is the relationship between the Old Testament and Christian faith. Christ is presented as the key to understanding the Old Testament Scriptures (see 1:1–4; 2:5–9). The church is the wandering people of God in search of heavenly rest and will find it if it persists in faith and obedience (3:7—4:11; 11:13–16). Christ is the genuine high priest, and the Old Testament cult was but a shadow of the worship that he would institute (5:1–10). The institutions of the old covenant and indeed the old covenant itself were copies and shadows of the true heavenly realities (8:1–13). The author's method of interpreting the Old Testament is typology; that is, the characters and institutions of the old covenant are used as prefigurations of the Christian dispensation. Though the precise situation of the sermon is not entirely clear, the addressees appear to be experiencing a crisis of some sort and stand in need of a "word of exhortation" (13:22).

First, Christ as the key to the Scriptures. The Old Testament revelation is assumed in Heb. 1:1 as authentic ("God spoke of old to our fathers"), but the revelation that has come through Jesus "in these last days" is seen as far superior in that he is the wisdom of God ("he reflects the glory of God and bears the very stamp of his nature, upholding the universe by his word of power"). As the wisdom of God, Jesus unlocks the mysteries of the Scriptures. So in Heb. 2:5–9, Ps. 8:4–6 with its talk about the "son of man" and his being made lower than the angels for a while and his being granted domination over all things is interpreted on the assumption that the Old Testament was really talking about Jesus. The author explains that while everything has been subjected to Christ, we do not see it yet. The "little while" in which he was lower than the angels is identified as Jesus' passion and death. His death had a value for everyone, and Jesus is aptly described as "the pioneer of their salvation" (2:10). As in Gal. 3:6–29, so here and indeed all through Hebrews the author tries to show that the Old Testament Scriptures become intelligible only when read in the light of Christ and his people.

Second, the church as the wandering people of God.[7] In Heb. 3:7—4:11 the author takes ancient Israel's wanderings in the wilderness as the type of the Christian community's present existence and uses them as a challenge to do better than Israel of old did. Whereas the Israel of old sought rest in the land of Canaan, the church now should seek heavenly rest. Whereas Israel of old did not find true rest because of its disbelief and disobedience, the church will find rest if it persists in faith and obedience (see also 1 Cor. 10:1–13). The author begins his presentation by quoting Ps. 95:7–11, which describes Israel's wanderings in the wilderness after the Exodus and prior to its entrance into Canaan:

> [7] Therefore, as the Holy Spirit says,
>   "Today, when you hear his voice,
> [8] do not harden your hearts as in the rebellion,
>   on the day of testing in the wilderness,
> [9] where your fathers put me to the test
>   and saw my works for forty years.
> [10] Therefore I was provoked with that generation,
>   and said, 'They always go astray in their hearts;
>   they have not known my ways.'
> [11] As I swore in my wrath,
>   'They shall never enter my rest.' "

The wandering of the Old Testament people of God is viewed as a time of punishment for Israel's rebellion against God and testing of his patience. Because of Israel's rebelliousness God grew angry at his people and swore that they would not find rest in the land of Canaan. That generation had to die off before Joshua could lead the people into the promised land.

In the commentary on Ps. 95:7–11 the author defines the crisis facing the community in terms of falling away from the living God (3:12) and urges the community to take the present opportunity ("today") to remain firm in Christ (3: 14). The rebellion of Israel of old is described in terms of disobedience and unbelief (3:18–19). Then the author argues that faith is the means by which one enters into rest (4:1–2) and that God's "rest" is a share in God's own Sabbath rest (that is, in heaven) and not the land of Canaan (4:3–5). See also Heb. 11:13–16 where the real goal of the patriarchs' wanderings as "strangers and exiles on the earth" is specified as the heavenly country prepared by God for them. Heb. 4:

6–11 makes it clear that the Christians as God's people in Christ rather than the Exodus generation are meant to enter God's rest. The Exodus generation failed to enter it because of its disobedience, but "today" it remains a possibility for the Christians. The psalm was not talking about Joshua and those who followed him into Canaan, for "there remains a sabbath rest for the people of God" (v. 9). So this commentary on Ps. 95:7–11 views the Christian community as God's people on a journey or pilgrimage toward life with God. It must profit from the negative example of Exodus generation's failure to find rest.

Third, Christ as the genuine high priest.[8] Using the Old Testament priesthood as a model, the author describes what a high priest does: "to act on behalf of men in relation to God, to offer gifts and sacrifices for sins" (5:1). He is chosen from among the people (5:1) but ultimately is called by God after the pattern of Aaron (5:4). He is able to sympathize with sinners and offers sacrifices for his own sins and those of the people (5:2–3). Having established the nature of the high priesthood, the author then proceeds to apply that definition to Christ and focuses on his call from God and his ability to sympathize with others. In 5:5–6 he uses the combination of Ps. 2:7 ("Thou art my Son, today I have begotten thee") and Ps. 110:4 ("Thou art a priest for ever, after the order of Melchizedek") to show that Christ was appointed by God. With little concern for the original meaning of the psalm texts, the author assumes that the calling of God's "anointed one" provides a pattern that finds its fullness in Christ. Once more we see at work the hermeneutical principle that Christ is the key to understanding the Old Testament and that all the Scriptures are directed toward him. Then in 5:7–8 Christ's ability to sympathize with others is grounded in the sufferings that he endured during his life on earth. The author carefully avoids saying that Jesus sinned (see 4:15), but insists that by suffering he has been qualified as the high priest and so has become "the source of eternal salvation to all who obey him" (5:9).

Fourth, the institutions of the old covenant. Heb. 8:1–2

uses the language of Ps. 110:1 ("The Lord said to my lord: 'Sit at my right hand, till I make your enemies your footstool' ") to express the royal and priestly roles of Jesus. Since Christ the high priest has been exalted to God's right hand, the sanctuary in which he officiates as high priest is a heavenly one. The tabernacle or tent that Moses was instructed to set up in the wilderness is viewed as but a shadow of the tabernacle set up in heaven where the exalted Jesus serves as high priest. Jesus the heavenly priest is not the same as those earthly priests who offer sacrifices in the tabernacle or the temple (8:3–4). Indeed the Old Testament institutions surrounding the priesthood were "a copy and shadow of the heavenly sanctuary" (v. 5). The concept of earthly institutions as shadows of eternal realities seems Platonic, but the author is careful to anchor the idea in the Old Testament notion of the "pattern" shown to Moses for furnishing the tabernacle in the wilderness: "And see that you make them after the pattern for them, which is being shown you on the mountain" (Exod. 25:40). Then in Heb. 8:6 the author roots the superior nature of Christ's priesthood in the superior nature of the new covenant, and the superior nature of the new covenant in the superior nature of the promises on which it is enacted. The idea of an old covenant being supplanted by a new covenant is then traced back to Jer. 31:31–34 in Heb. 8:8–12, and the argument concludes by declaring the first covenant "obsolete" and by adding, "what is becoming obsolete and growing old is ready to vanish away" (8:13). Whereas Paul in Romans 9—11 took pains to avoid the old covenant–new covenant antithesis and sought a real place for unbelieving Israel in his vision of God's plan of salvation, the author of Hebrews dismisses the faith and activities of unbelieving Israel as obsolete and soon to vanish. At most the old covenant was a shadow and a type of the new covenant (see also Heb. 7:12, 18–19; 10:1, 9).

REVELATION

Usually considered as having been composed in the latter part of the emperor Domitian's reign (A.D. 81–96), the Book of Revelation reflects an atmosphere in which the churches in Asia Minor were about to suffer persecution or were indeed already enduring it at the hands of the state. The seer in 1:19 has been given the task of writing down what he has seen (1:9–20), what is (1:1–8; 2:1—3:22), and what is to take place hereafter (4:1—22:21). Even a glance at this rough outline shows the extent to which the author of Revelation wishes "to turn the reader's eyes from the tribulations of the present to a glorious future, so that he might remain faithful and have the prospect of being acquitted at the judgment and of sharing in salvation."[9] The readers of Revelation are urged not to take up arms in active resistance, not even in the final eschatological battle. They are to endure persecution including death and to hope for ultimate salvation (see chap. 12; also 2:10; 13:10), though 6:9–11 suggests that the death of each martyr does bring the Day of the Lord closer.[10]

What kind of religious ideology does the author of Revelation provide for the churches of Asia in their time of crisis? Like the authors of 1 Peter and Hebrews, the seer of Revelation draws upon Jewish traditions on the assumption that these are fully intelligible now when applied to the church. So the vision of the hundred and forty-four thousand marked with seals in chap. 7 is built upon the tradition of the twelve tribes of Israel, and the "heavenly woman" in the vision of chap. 12 wears a crown of twelve stars. The identification of the woman's offspring as "those who keep the commandments of God and bear testimony to Jesus" (12:17) indicates that in the background of this enigmatic passage is the equation between the woman symbolizing the people of God and the church. But in this section I would like to concentrate on those three passages in Revelation (1:6; 5:10; 20:6) in which Christians are called priests. In 1 Pet. 2:9 the Christian community was described as a "royal priesthood," and in Heb. 5:1–10 Christ was presented as the high priest presiding over the heavenly cult. Here we want to know how the readers of the Book of Revelation can be called "priests to God."[11]

A clear understanding of two Old Testament passages in

which the term "priests" is applied to Israel (Exod. 19:6; Isa.
61:6) is necessary for interpreting the three texts in Revelation. In the section on 1 Peter we have already treated the
phrase in Exod. 19:6 "a kingdom of priests and a holy nation." Israel's status as a royal priesthood (or a kingdom and
priests)[12] is said to depend on its fidelity to the covenant relationship with God. The idea seems to be that if Israel is faithful to the covenant it will be set apart like priests from the
profane world and will be especially close to God. The second
text (Isa. 61:6) occurs in a poem of hope for what is going to
take place when Israel returns to its land from the Babylonian
exile: "Aliens shall stand and feed your flocks, foreigners shall
be your plowmen and vinedressers, but you shall be called the
priests of the Lord, men shall speak of you as the ministers of
our God." Here Israel as a group is promised a special status
vis-à-vis other peoples. At the root of the passage are the
special privileges accorded to the tribe of Levi with respect to
the other tribes (see Deut. 18:1–5). In the glorious return
from the Exile Israel's status among the nations will be anal-
ogous to that of the Levites among the twelve tribes. Just as
the Levites have a particular place in Israel, so Israel will have
a particular place among the nations of the world.

In 1 Pet. 2:5, 9 the Christian community is called a "priesthood" (*hierateuma*).[13] The expression alludes to Exod. 19:6
and is used to describe the elect character and the holiness of
the corporate people of God. Just as Israel on Sinai was constituted the priestly corporation charged with the task of
maintaining holiness in the world, so the church made up of
Jews and Gentiles now carries out this commission. The understanding of the church's priesthood in Revelation is a little
different from the essentially corporate notion in 1 Peter.[14]
Both Rev. 1:6 and 5:10 call all those redeemed by Christ
"priests" instead of a "priesthood" and seem to envision the
individual Christian as a priest (*hiereus*). In 1:5–6 Jesus
Christ is praised as "him who loves us and has freed us from
our sins by his blood and made us a kingdom, priests to his
God and Father." Perhaps part of a baptismal formula, this

passage views Christ as installing the redeemed as people in
power ("kingdom") and priests (*hiereis*). Rev. 5:9–10 is a
liturgical fragment in which "the saints" praise the Lamb
(Christ) for having ransomed persons "from every tribe and
tongue and people and nation" and making them "a kingdom
and priests (*hiereis*) to our God." Christ's death has saving
power for all peoples and has made them a kingdom and
priests. Both texts in Revelation depend upon Exod. 19:6, but
the Greek version of the Hebrew text that they presume joins
an abstract term "kingdom" and a masculine plural noun
"priests." Whereas "priesthood" in 1 Pet. 2:5, 9 is clearly a
collective term, "priests" in Rev. 1:6 and 5:10 suggests that
individual Christians can be called priests.

The third "priestly" text in Revelation occurs in 20:6,
which speaks of a future judgment to be rendered for those
Christians who have suffered martyrdom, especially for refus-
ing to take part in the pagan cult. In their thousand-year reign
with Christ "they shall be priests of God and of Christ." The
martyrs are said to be priests (*hiereis*) in some eschatological
time. Most interpreters see this passage as based on Isa. 61:6,
which says that in the future Israel will be to the nations as
the Levites are to the rest of Israel. Rev. 20:4–6 swarms with
problems of interpretation, but this much is clear: the priesthood is not granted so much to the church as community (see
1 Pet. 2:5, 9) but to the martyrs who have not worshiped
"the beast." Furthermore, the passage envisions a priesthood
that reaches full realization in the eschatological future. This
future note had previously been sounded in Rev. 5:10 ("and
they shall reign on earth") but is absent in 1:6. Are the
martyrs priests in the future or in the present? Also, why is a
priesthood needed in the eschaton?

The serious problems encountered in interpreting Rev. 1:6;
5:10; 20:6 should not distract us from the basic point: individuals "from every tribe and tongue and people and nation"
have been shaped by Christ into a priestly people after the
pattern of ancient Israel. Ethnic origin is no bar to being part
of God's people in Christ, and that people plays the role in

the world at large previously played by Israel. An ideology drawing on the Jewish tradition of Israel as a priestly people is invoked to sustain this Christian community in its present trials in the largely pagan milieu of Asia Minor.

CONCLUSION

In 1 Peter, Hebrews, and Revelation we have seen examples of early Christian communities that dealt with their status as minority groups within the Hellenistic culture surrounding them by appropriating to themselves aspects of ancient Israel's self-consciousness. Despite their being strangers and aliens in this world, these early Christians viewed history as the proper arena for being the people of God (1 Peter), for the people's pilgrimage toward "rest" with God (Hebrews), and for being priests of God and Christ (Revelation). There is little indication that these were entirely or even predominantly Jewish-Christian groups. Indeed what indications there are suggest that they were mixed or largely Gentile-Christian churches (certainly in 1 Peter). Yet each author thought that invoking the Old Testament concept of the people of God was an appropriate way of responding to the social and political crises confronting his community. The three documents treated here provide vivid testimony to the importance of this complex of thought in early Christianity's self-consciousness. They also raise the possibility that the idea of the church as God's people in Christ is not limited to converts from Judaism. Rather it seems to be part of Christianity's enduring self-consciousness regardless of the ethnic origin or the social setting of the individual community.

NOTES

1. J. H. Elliott, "The Rehabilitation of an Exegetical Step-Child: 1 Peter in Recent Research," *JBL* 95 (1976): 243–54.

2. C. J. Hemer, "The Address of 1 Peter," *ExpTim* 89 (1978): 239–43.

3. V. P. Furnish, "Elect Sojourners in Christ: An Approach to the Theology of I Peter," *Perkins Journal* 28 (1975): 1–11.

4. N. Brox, "Situation und Sprache der Minderheit im ersten Petrusbrief," *Kairos* 19 (1977): 1–13.

5. C. Wolff, "Christ und Welt im 1. Petrusbrief," *TLZ* 100 (1975): 333–42.

6. W. G. Kümmel, *Introduction to the New Testament*, trans. H. C. Kee (Nashville and New York: Abingdon Press, 1975), pp. 398–401.

7. E. Käsemann, *Das wandernde Gottesvolk: Eine Untersuchung zum Hebräerbrief*, FRLANT 55 (Göttingen: Vandenhoeck & Ruprecht, 1939).

8. W. G. Johnsson, "The Cultus of Hebrews in Twentieth-Century Scholarship," *ExpTim* 89 (1978): 104–8. See also his "Issues in the Interpretation of Hebrews," *AUSS* 15 (1977): 169–87.

9. W. Marxsen, *Introduction to the New Testament: An Approach to Its Problems*, trans. G. Buswell (Philadelphia: Fortress Press, 1968), p. 275.

10. A. Y. Collins, "The Political Perspective of the Revelation to John," *JBL* 96 (1977): 241–56.

11. E. Schüssler-Fiorenza, *Priester für Gott: Studien zum Herrschafts- und Priestermotiv in der Apokalypse*, NTAbh n.s. 7 (Münster: Aschendorff, 1972). See my review in *CBQ* 34 (1972): 496–97.

12. The Hebrew phrase *mamleket kōhănîm* can be interpreted as either "a kingdom of priests" or "a kingdom, priests." The Greek of the Septuagint (*basileion hierateuma*) can be translated as "a royal priesthood" or "kingdom, priesthood."

13. J. H. Elliott, *The Elect and the Holy: An Exegetical Examination of 1 Peter 2:4–10 and the Phrase* basileion hierateuma, NovTSup 12 (Leiden: Brill, 1966).

14. E. Schüssler-Fiorenza, *Priester für Gott.*

CHAPTER 8

Jesus as the
Focus of the Conflict
with the Synagogue

The Gospels of Matthew and John constitute something of a paradox within the New Testament. They are far more interested in the Jewishness of Jesus and in Jewish institutions than the Gospels of Mark and Luke are, but their apparently "anti-Jewish" statements have furnished anti-Semites through the ages with dangerous ammunition. Moreover, everything in these Gospels indicates that the evangelists themselves were of Jewish origin and that a great part of their communities were Jewish Christians. How can these Gospels written by Jews for largely Jewish-Christian communities have had the perverse effect of fostering anti-Jewish sentiments?

The answer to this question is to be found in the historical settings in which these documents were put into final form. Both Gospels seem to have been composed after the destruction of Jerusalem and its temple in A.D. 70 and after various Jewish groups including the early Christians had wrestled with the question, who or where is Israel now that the temple is no more and its rebuilding in the immediate future appears unlikely? Matthew and John give the same response: Israel now is the church gathered around Jesus Christ. Once more the central significance of Christology for understanding the church as the people of God emerges. The people of God is constituted in and through Jesus Christ, and surely one of the primary reasons that these evangelists wrote their Gospels was to give concrete meaning to the church's claim to be the people of God in Christ.

This chapter has two parts. The first part will explore the historical setting of Matthew's Gospel, its use of the Old Testament, the Matthean rewriting of the parable of the vineyard, and the scathing critique of the scribes and Pharisees in chap. 23. The second part examines the exclusion of the Johannine Christians from the synagogue, the charges made concerning Jesus by the leaders of the synagogue, the Johannine reinterpretation of the Jewish festal calendar, and the portrayal of "the Jews" in the Fourth Gospel. Attention to these matters will shed light on the conflicts between Jewish Christians and other Jews in the late first century and will provide us today with a historical framework for evaluating the so-called anti-Jewish statements in the Gospels of Matthew and John.

MATTHEW

Matthew's Gospel was put into final form perhaps in Antioch of Syria around A.D. 85; that is, after the Christian community had existed for about fifty years since Jesus' death and after the Jerusalem temple had been destroyed for approximately fifteen years. This dating is based to a large extent on what seems to be a description of the events of A.D. 70 in Jerusalem: "The king was angry, and he sent his troops and destroyed these murderers and burned their city" (Matt. 22: 7). The Matthean community was a mixed group, but the majority apparently was Jewish Christian.[1] By A.D. 85 it had become clear that not all Israel was going to become Christian and that the most promising missionary field was the Gentiles: "Go therefore and make disciples of all the Gentiles" (28: 19).[2] Matthew was encouraging a predominantly Jewish-Christian community to recognize itself as the legitimate heir to God's promises to Israel and to broaden out its missionary horizons to include the Gentiles. There is, however, no suggestion of Paul's strategy of making Israel jealous by means of the Gentile mission.

For fifteen years or so the religious and political center of Judaism had been destroyed. The heart of Jewish piety—the temple—had ceased to function, and all Judaism had to answer the question, Who is the true Israel?[3] Apocalyptists like the authors of 4 Ezra and 2 Baruch clung to the hope that those who remain faithful in the present tribulation will finally be rewarded when God's kingdom comes. Political revolutionaries like the Zealots continued the armed struggle for a while only to go down to defeat at Masada. Law-oriented Jews like the scribes and Pharisees joined Yohanan ben Zakkai in his rabbinical academy at Yavneh (Jamnia) by the Mediterranean coast and devoted themselves to the understanding and observance of the biblical statutes and the traditions surrounding them. Christians like Matthew answered that the church is now "the true Israel" in that Jesus of Nazareth is the Messiah of Jewish expectation and the fulfillment of the Old Testament promises.

The radical change in Judaism brought about by the destruction of the temple in A.D. 70 cannot be overlooked if we are to grasp the setting in life of Matthew's Gospel. Temple-oriented Judaism had come to an end, and both rabbinic Judaism and Christianity were bold and upstart responses to the question about the present identity of God's people. Matthew asserts that the Christian church is the true Israel and attempts to define that church over against rival claims within Judaism. The most serious rival seems to have been the Pharisaic movement. By the time of the Gospel's composition, Christians of Jewish origin no longer belong to "their synagogues" (4:23; 9:35; 10:17; 12:9; 13:54), which are also called the synagogues of the hypocrites (6:2, 5; 23:6, 34).

Matthew gives validity to his claim that Jesus fulfills the biblical promises by his many "formula quotations" and by his portrayal of Jesus as the authoritative interpreter of the Law. A formula quotation is a citation of a specific Old Testament text accompanied by an introductory phrase such as "all this took place to fulfill what the Lord had spoken through the prophet." These formula quotations are especially prominent in the infancy narrative (Matt. 1—2) as a means of confirming the extraordinary nature of Jesus' birth (1:23) and his itinerary as a child (2:15, 18, 23). They are also used in connection with Jesus' ministry in Galilee (4:15–16), his healing activities (8:17), his role as the servant of God (12:18–21), his use of parables (13:35), his entrance into Jerusalem on Palm Sunday (21:5), his arrest (26:56), and his betrayal by Judas (27:9–10). Matthew's hermeneutical principle is basically the same as Paul's in Galatians 3: Christ is the key that unlocks the mysteries of the Old Testament Scriptures. Not only does Jesus' life fulfill the Old Testament, but also his teaching is portrayed by Matthew as the authoritative interpretation of the Law and the prophets: "I have come not to abolish them but to fulfill them" (5:17). The six antitheses (5:21–48) present commandments from the Old Testament ("you have heard that it was said to the men of old") regarding homicide, adultery, divorce, swearing falsely, retaliation, and love of neighbor. The citations are accompanied by Jesus' own teaching on the matters ("but I say to you") in which he either extends the commandment's scope by going to the root of the abuse or abrogates the commandment in the cases of divorce and oaths permitted by the Law. The presentation of Jesus' life as fulfilling prophecies and of his teaching as the authoritative interpretation of the Law would have been very important to a largely Jewish-Christian community like Matthew's in its effort to justify its claim to be God's people.

An allegory is a comparison in which each detail is meaningful and each feature stands for something. Approximately ninety years of critical analysis of the Gospel parables have taught us that these narratives generally have only one point (usually the kingdom of God) and are not to be interpreted as allegories. But the parable of the vineyard in Mark 12:1–11 comes very close to being an allegory. The very beginning of the narrative ("A man planted a vineyard, and set a hedge around it, and dug a pit for the winepress, and built a tower, and let it out to tenants") is so shot through with allusions to Isaiah's song of the vineyard (Isa. 5:1–7) that an identification of the vineyard and Israel seems inescapable ("the vineyard of the Lord of hosts is the house of Israel, and the men of Judah are his pleasant planting"). As the story develops, a web of allegorical features is woven: the owner is God; the tenants are the political and religious leaders of Israel; the servants sent to the vineyard are the prophets; and the beloved son is Christ. The parable of the vineyard places the rejection of Jesus by Israel in the tradition of its rejection of the prophets. Matt. 21:33–43 takes over the basic Marcan story line of the parable of the vineyard but makes two very important additions in vv. 41 and 43. In v. 41 Matthew rewrites Mark's version of what the owner of the vineyard will do as a response to the tenants' murder of his beloved son: "He will put those wretches to a miserable death, and let out the vineyard to other tenants who will give him the fruits in their season." Clearly the men of Judah are no longer God's "pleasant planting" of Isa. 5:7. The Matthean verse alludes to the destruction of Jerusalem in A.D. 70 and interprets that catastrophe as divine judgment on "the men of Judah." Also envisioned is the transfer of Israel's religious patrimony as the vineyard of God to another group, to the other tenants who will give him the fruits in their season. Given the fact that the Matthean ideal of discipleship is "bearing fruit" (see Matt. 7:15–20), there can be no doubt that "the other tenants" are the Christians. Then by way of conclusion to the parable (v. 43), Matthew adds the comment, "Therefore I tell you, the kingdom of God will be taken away from you and given to a nation producing the fruits of it." The elect status of Israel as the recipients of the coming kingdom of God has been taken away and given to a new *ethnos* made up of Jews and Gentiles who confess Jesus as the Messiah. The point of the special Matthean material in vv. 41 and 43 is that "the men of Judah" and those who claim to be in closest continuity with them (the scribes and Pharisees, the rabbis) no longer have a valid claim to the title "people of God." Instead of them, the Christians (whatever their racial origins) constitute the "nation" (*ethnos*) that confesses Christ as the fulfillment of the Old Testament hopes and produces fruits in their actions. So Matthew has used the parable of the vineyard to confirm his claim that church is the people of God in Christ.

The critique of the scribes and Pharisees in Matthew 23 has become an embarrassment to Christian theologians in their dialogues with Jewish representatives. All too often in Christian history this passage has served as a mine of anti-Jewish stereotypes and as a goad toward verbal and physical attacks against Jews. Once more the passage becomes readily intelligible when looked at from a historical-critical perspective. A glance at a synopsis of the Gospels will show that the passage has few parallels in Mark or Luke. It consists mainly of special Matthean material. A look at the structure of Matthew's Gospel as a whole will reveal that "the woes" against the scribes and Pharisees occur at the beginning of the fifth large block of speech material (chaps. 5—7; 10; 13; 18; 23—25). The first speech begins with the beatitudes ("blessed are the poor in spirit"), and the last speech begins with the warnings ("woe to you, scribes and Pharisees"). Comparison of the content of the passage with what we know about the teachings of the earthly Jesus casts doubt on the attribution of much of the material gathered and presented here to Jesus. Considerations of sources, literary technique, and content all suggest that most of Matthew 23 in its present form should be interpreted primarily as reflecting the post–A.D. 70 struggle between the church and the synagogue over the claim to be God's people. The scribes and Pharisees are criticized for imposing burdens on others and failing to carry out their own teachings (vv. 3–4), for ostentatiousness in the practices of piety (vv. 5–7), for closing up the kingdom of God (v. 13), for hypocritical zeal in making proselytes (v. 15), for swearing oaths (vv. 16–22), for neglecting the truly important parts of the Law (vv. 23–24), for being inwardly full of vice (vv. 25–28), and for killing the prophets (vv. 29–39). While some of this material may go back to the earthly Jesus, the form in which it now appears in Matthew 23 tells us more about the conflict between the church and "their synagogues" after A.D. 70 than it does about the earthly Jesus.

How are these polemics in Matthew 23 to be evaluated today?[4] Obviously the charge of anti-Semitism is not applicable, since Matthew and a large part of his community were Jews and saw themselves as squarely within the Jewish tradition. The explanation that these polemics were aimed only at the Jewish leaders has some truth to it, but presumably the critique included those who followed such leaders (see 27:25 where the whole people [*laos*] takes upon itself the guilt for Jesus' passion and death). Nor is there much evidence for these polemics as being a pedagogical device designed to shock unbelieving Israel into action. Rather they must be read as part of the Matthean community's struggle with other groups in Judaism as to who inherits the religious tradition of Israel. Matthew and his community have separated from the synagogue and are defining themselves over against Pharisaic Judaism and its adherents.[5] The so-called anti-Jewish passages come from a predominantly Jewish community that makes its claim to be God's people primarily in terms of Jesus the Messiah and secondarily by criticizing its rivals as hypocrites. The heat of the polemic may be due to affronts suffered by Christians, but there is no trace of urging Christians toward offensive or violent actions against the opponents. In fact, the Christians are urged to pray for their persecutors (5:12) and to love their enemies (5:44–47). The polemic may also be designed as a warning to Christians to avoid the faults of their "hypocritical" rivals.

JOHN

During the past decade research on the Fourth Gospel has concentrated especially on developing a history of the Johannine community and on trying to understand the issues confronting that community.[6] Two major themes have emerged. First, it appears that John's Gospel was written after members of the community had been expelled from the synagogue. This line of research has focused especially on the so-called Book of Signs in chaps. 1—12. The second theme involves the relation of the later church to Jesus and to the first generation of disciples. When the Fourth Gospel was put into final form around A.D.

90, a major issue was how the community was to continue without Jesus and his disciples.[7] The material in the so-called Book of Glory in chaps. 13—20 has been the focus of attention in this area of study. It is interesting to observe that Matthew and John are facing the same set of problems: the relation of the church to the synagogue after A.D. 70 and the relation of Christians in the community to Christ and to one another.

The history of the Johannine community is getting very complicated. There is an increasing tendency to see the so-called beloved disciple as a disciple of the earthly Jesus and as the founder of the Johannine school.[8] Within the religious purview of the Gospel itself one of its most distinguished commentators has now discerned six different groups: the "Jews," the crypto-Christians, the Jewish Christians, Christians of apostolic churches, the Johannine Christians, and the secessionist Johannine Christians.[9] When the Gospel was written, the Johannine Christians were defining themselves over against the other groups. Our concern here is the tension between the Johannine community and the "Jews" who remain faithful to the synagogue as seen in the Book of Signs.

The most extensive and coherent treatment of the tension between church and synagogue in John is J. Louis Martyn's *History and Theology in the Fourth Gospel*.[10] Martyn's basic thesis is that the material in the Book of Signs (chaps. 1—12) is to be read on two levels—both as stories about Jesus and as stories about the state of the Johannine community around A.D. 90. He argues that in the course of the Johannine community's development a collection of miracle stories (the signs of Jesus) was expanded and rewritten as advice for the present situation; that is, after the Christians had been expelled from the synagogue. As in the case of Matthew's Gospel, the stories in the Fourth Gospel probably tell us more about the evangelist's situation than about the earthly Jesus.

The prime example of this approach comes in the middle of the story of the healing of the man born blind in chap. 9. After recounting the healing itself in vv. 1–7, the passage consists of a series of dialogues between the healed man and his neighbors (8–12), the man and the Pharisees (13–17), between the Jews and the man's parents (18–23) and the man (24–34), and between Jesus and the man (35–38) and the Pharisees (39–41). The key passage comes in the dialogue between the Jews and the man's parents: "His parents said this because they feared the Jews, for the Jews had already agreed that if anyone should confess him to be Christ, he was to be put out of the synagogue" (v. 22). The use of the expression "out of the synagogue" (*aposynagōgos*) seems to reflect a formal decision on the part of the Jewish officials that Christians were to be excluded from their fellowship within the synagogue. This term *aposynagōgos* occurs only in two other New Testament passages, both of them in John's Gospel. In 12:42 we hear that many of the authorities believed in Jesus but "for fear of the Pharisees they did not confess it, lest they should be put out of the synagogue." In 16:2 Jesus warns his disciples of the troubles ahead: "They will put you out of the synagogues." These three instances of the expression "out of the synagogue" indicate that exclusion from this institution was an important concern within the Johannine community. This sharp division between church and synagogue is confirmed in John 9:28 when the Jews revile the man with the words, "You are his disciple, but we are disciples of Moses." Just as in Matthew there is a split between the church and "their synagogues," so here there is a division between the disciples of Jesus and the disciples of Moses.

Another incident in the Book of Signs that is especially relevant to the tension between the Johannine Christians and the Jews of the synagogue is the healing of the sick man by the pool of Beth-Zatha (or Bethesda) in chap. 5. After the actual healing (vv. 2–9b), the Jews question the man in a hostile manner, but Jesus assures him that no evil will befall him (9c–15). Then vv. 16–18 present the twofold charge made by the Jews against Jesus: "he not only broke the sabbath but also called God his Father, making himself equal with God." Observance of the sabbath and the claims made about the person of Jesus seem to have been precisely the issues that led to the exclusion of the Christians from the synagogue. In John 7:12 the opponents are quoted as saying that Jesus "is leading the people astray." These two texts (5:18 and 7:12) are further evidence that in the Book of Signs we have expansions and rewritings of traditions about Jesus against the background of the expulsion of Christians from what had become the central religious institution of Judaism after A.D. 70.

The hypothesis that the Book of Signs reflects the struggle between church and synagogue after A.D. 70 is confirmed by a glance at the structure of chaps. 2—10.[11] In chaps. 2—4 Jesus is active in the major geographical areas of Palestine: Galilee (2:1–12), Jerusalem (2:13—4:3), Samaria (4:4–45), and Galilee again (4:46–54). In chaps. 5—10 the Jewish festal calendar provides the principle of organization. On the Sabbath (5:9) Jesus by healing the man at the pool performs works that only God can do on that day. At Passover (6:4) Jesus himself replaces the manna of the Exodus by multiplying the loaves, and at Tabernacles (7:2) he replaces the water and light ceremonies of that feast. On the feast of the Rededication of the Temple or Hanukkah (10:22), Jesus as Messiah and Son of God is consecrated in place of the temple altar. In each incident in chaps. 5—10 the full meaning of an important Jewish holy day is found in the person of Jesus. The fact that all these incidents are situated in the environs of the temple at Jerusalem indicates that the Jewish festival calendar, now that the temple had been destroyed, is best carried on in the community of Jesus Christ. The dynamic in the Book of Signs is similar to that in Matthew's Gospel and in many other New Testament writings: Jesus Christ is the decisive point of reference in forming the new people of God, and the true children of Abraham (8:31–47) and Jacob (4:10–15) are those who heed the words of Jesus as the one sent from God.

One of the prominent features of the Fourth Gospel is its use of the term "the Jews" in a negative or hostile sense. Though sometimes the expression merely has a geographical sense ("the Judeans") or a neutral sense ("the festival of the

Jews"),[12] it frequently (as in the texts from chaps. 5 and 9 of the Book of Signs discussed above) describes a group of opponents allied with the world and the powers of evil against Jesus and his flock. Whereas the synoptic tradition specifies various groups of opponents (Pharisees, Sadducees, Herodians, chief priests), John tends to lump them all together as "the Jews." It is important to read these passages about "the Jews" against the background of the exclusion of Jewish Christians from the synagogue and the emergence of the church as a sociologically distinct institution. It is also important to recognize that once the Gospel with its hostile references to "the Jews" was circulated among Gentile Christians it acquired an anti-Semitic potential that has been abundantly and tragically actualized in the course of Christian history.[13]

CONCLUSION

What dimensions of the church's claim to be the people of God emerge out of the Gospels of Matthew and John? Both Gospels reflect a historical setting after the destruction of the Jerusalem temple in A.D. 70 when the identity of Israel as God's people in its traditional sense had been dramatically called into question. Both Gospels anchor the Christian claim to be God's people in the person of Jesus. For Matthew, Jesus fulfills the Old Testament Scriptures and serves as their authoritative interpreter. For John, the Jewish calendar of holy days finds its true meaning in Christ and is best observed with reference to him. The most blatant "anti-Jewish" passages in both Gospels suppose the exclusion of Jewish Christians from the synagogue and are part of the church's claim to be God's people in opposition to rival claims to the title being made by other Jewish groups. Nevertheless, neither Matthew nor John yet sees the Christian community as a new religion apart from Judaism. Their anger is over the exclusion of their community from the synagogue. Paradoxically, then, despite their strong anti-Jewish statements, they are eloquent testimony to the radical Jewishness of early Christian self-understanding.

NOTES

1. D. J. Harrington, "Matthean Studies Since Joachim Rohde," *HeyJ* 16 (1975): 375–88.

2. D. R. A. Hare and D. J. Harrington, " 'Make Disciples of All the Gentiles' (Matthew 28:19)," *CBQ* 37 (1975): 359–69.

3. J. Neusner, "Judaism in a Time of Crisis: Four Responses to the Destruction of the Second Temple," *Judaism* 21 (1972): 313–27.

4. S. Légasse, "L' 'anti-judaisme' dans l'Évangile selon Matthieu," in *L'Évangile selon Matthieu: Rédaction et théologie,* ed. M. Didier, BETL 29 (Gembloux: Duculot, 1972), pp. 417–28.

5. D. R. A. Hare, *The Theme of Jewish Persecution of Christians in the Gospel according to St. Matthew,* SNTSMS 6 (New York and London: Cambridge University Press, 1967).

6. R. Kysar, "Community and Gospel: Vectors in Fourth Gospel Criticism," *Int* 31 (1977): 355–66.

7. P. S. Minear, "The Audience of the Fourth Gospel," *Int* 31 (1977): 339–54.

8. O. Cullmann, *The Johannine Circle,* trans. J. Bowden (Philadelphia: Westminster Press, 1976).

9. R. E. Brown, " 'Other Sheep not of this Fold': The Johannine Perspective on Christian Diversity in the Late First Century," *JBL* 97 (1978): 5–22. See also idem, *The Community of the Beloved Disciple* (New York, Ramsey, and Toronto: Paulist Press, 1979).

10. J. L. Martyn, *History and Theology in the Fourth Gospel,* 2d ed. revised and enlarged (Nashville: Abingdon Press, 1979).

11. R. E. Brown, *The Gospel according to John (i-xii),* AB 29 (Garden City, N.Y.: Doubleday & Co., 1966), pp. CXL–CXLI.

12. M. Lowe, "Who were the *IOUDAIOI?*" *NovT* 18 (1976): 101–30.

13. R. H. Fuller, "The 'Jews' in the Fourth Gospel," *Dialog* 16 (1977): 31–37. See also R. Leistner, *Antijudaismus im Johannesevangelium? Darstellung des Problems in der neueren Auslegungsgeschichte und Untersuchung der Leidensgeschichte,* Theologie und Wirklichkeit 3 (Bern: H. Lang, 1974).

CHAPTER 9

Challenges for
the Church Today

This book has presented a description of early Christianity's attempts at defining itself with reference to Judaism. Attention to representative Old Testament passages has revealed important dimensions of Israel's sense of being God's people: divinely initiated, historical, and covenantal. A glance at some postexilic texts showed that these ideas continued to exercise great influence, though special emphasis was placed on observing particular commandments or belonging to particular groups. In the context of belonging to God's people, Jesus of Nazareth preached about the future and present aspects of the kingdom. Those gathered around Jesus in life and death looked very much like other Jewish apocalyptic communities of their time but were distinguished from them primarily by faith in Jesus' death and resurrection as God's decisive intervention in human history.

Paul's position that "if you are Christ's, then you are Abraham's offspring" (Gal. 3:29) constituted a major breakthrough. It encouraged those who were not born as Jews to share in the religious heritage of Israel by means of incorporation into Christ. Membership in God's people was now defined in religious rather than ethnic terms. In Romans 9—11 Paul argued that all who accept Christ in faith—whether they are Jews or Gentiles by origin—are the real children of Abraham. Nevertheless, he also saw a place within God's plan of salvation for those Israelites who did not yet profess faith in Christ. The author of Ephesians stressed that the people made up of Jews and Gentiles forms the body of Christ, that in and through Christ Jews and Gentiles have been shaped into a single people.

The other side of the "togetherness" in Christ so vigorously encouraged by Paul and the author of Ephesians was the tendency toward distinguishing the people of God in Christ from those Jews and Gentiles who were not in Christ. Some of the dynamics of this process appear in 1 Timothy: emphasis on sound doctrine, exemplary behavior as a missionary strategy, the idea of the church as God's household and the bulwark of truth, and the growing importance attached to church officials. The imagery connected with ancient Israel's sense of peoplehood was invoked by the authors of 1 Peter, Hebrews, and Revelation as a way of expressing the self-consciousness of the Christian community. The Gospels of Matthew and John reflect the struggles with other Jewish religious movements after A.D. 70 for the right to claim the heritage of Israel as God's own people.

Our biblical-theological investigation of the church as God's people in Christ has focused on specific texts in the hope of getting in touch with some decisive ecclesiological moments in the earliest stages of Christian history. The method has been exegetical and descriptive, and the result is a series of glimpses into some varieties of communal consciousness found in the biblical tradition. Perhaps other parts of the New Testament deserve further attention (for example, Luke-Acts),[1] and perhaps other aspects of the documents treated here (for example, the anti-Jewish character of the passion stories in the Gospels)[2] merit further examination. But enough exegesis has been presented and a sufficient variety of insights have been explored to leave the reader at this point asking about the overall theological significance of the study.

What does it mean to call the church "the people of God"? What are the most important challenges to the church today that emerge out of the individual analyses presented in this book? As I said in the opening chapter, I have no intention of gathering together all the relevant information about the church as the people of God and mixing it into one comprehensive doctrine of the church. Rather I will try to remain faithful to the thrusts of the particular texts studied here and will explore some of their ramifications for the life of the church today. After all, the Christian churches affirm that these biblical texts are authoritative in some way and therefore Christians take upon themselves the obligation to listen to the texts and act upon them. Indeed the statements about the church in the documents of the so-called apostolic period have furnished direction and vitality to the Christian community throughout the centuries. At a time in history when so many of the church's cultural moorings are being cut away and when people are legitimately concerned to know what is essential and what is accidental about the ways in which our churches operate, a serious reflection on the foundational documents of Christianity can only have a purifying and salutary effect. My concluding observations will be presented as a series of challenges to the church today that I think arise out of the biblical texts examined in the preceding chapters.

1. Israel's spiritual heritage. If the church is to carry on the spiritual heritage of the Old Testament people of God, it must see itself as graced and as called by God, must look to the events of history as a place of divine revelation, and must remain faithful to the covenantal structure of faith. In Galatians 3 and Romans 4, Paul insists that through Christ even Gentiles can become children of Abraham and part of God's people. A corollary to this claim is the idea that Abraham is the model or pattern of genuine Christian faith. According to the stories about Abraham presented in the Old Testament and treasured by the early Christians, Abraham left his homeland in response to God's call to him. Abraham's vocation was not to individual salvation or to personal growth but rather to stand at the head of a people with a God, a land, and a law. The vivid sense of belonging to a people, of solidarity with others, of being part of something larger than oneself—all this is involved in church's claim to be God's people in Christ. The Old Testament passages about the people of God do not claim this status for Israel because of Israel's own merits or its natural

abilities or its size. God's grace, and not Israel's achievements, is at the root of the people's identity: "It is because the Lord loves you" (Deut. 7:8). Likewise, the church's claim to be God's people must never degenerate into exclusionism or triumphalism, because whatever status it has before God is based entirely on God's initiative. Moreover, we saw that the Old Testament people of God looked upon the events of history, especially the Exodus from Egypt and the gift of the land of Canaan, as an arena for God's activity on its behalf. This same kind of commitment to think about and act upon the events of history from a religious point of view sustained the Jewish people through the triumphs and catastrophes of its later history and allowed the New Testament writers to discern in the life, death, and resurrection of Jesus of Nazareth God's most decisive intervention in human affairs. Whenever the church separates itself from the world in which it exists and pretends to have no interest in the events of its time, its claim to be God's people may be legitimately doubted. Finally, like Israel of old, the church stands in a covenant relationship with God. Recognizing the validity of God's claims over it, the church must seek to respond in ways that are appropriate to its identity as God's people in Christ. God's people in Christ as children of Abraham cannot neglect its spiritual roots and cannot avoid the challenges raised by the shape of Israel's peoplehood: the appreciation of God's grace, the obligation to discern the hand of God in our history, and the acknowledgment of God's covenantal lordship and of our status as his servants.

2. The centrality of Christ. The church's claim to be God's people is based entirely on the person of Jesus Christ. Jesus the Jew of Nazareth is the principle of continuity between Israel of old and the church. By confessing Jesus of Nazareth as the Messiah of Jewish expectation, the church affirms that it now carries on the Jewish spiritual heritage. Whereas the Qumran community saw the events involving its own group as the key that unlocked the mysteries of the Scriptures, early Christian interpreters like Luke, Paul, the author of Hebrews, and Matthew insisted that Christ is the key to the Scriptures. So im-

pressed with Jesus Christ were the early Christians that they confessed him as the vehicle for the fulfillment of God's promises to Israel. By nature Jesus belonged to God's people Israel, and this one Israelite has made it possible for individuals of all ethnic backgrounds to be part of that people.

Aren't we all God's people? Does not the mere fact of creation make us part of the people of God? Not exactly! When we use the term "the people of God," we refer to the mysterious special relationship existing between God and a certain segment of humanity that is the principal theme of the Bible. As I have previously emphasized, that special relationship is not based on merit or achievement but upon grace. If one accepts the Scriptures as authoritative documents, one also affirms that "a people of God" exists within the much larger expanse of humanity. The issue that confronted the early church was this: How do individuals enter that special relationship with God? The answer provided by Paul and those who followed his lead was that one enters the special communal relationship with God in and through Jesus Christ. Jesus of Nazareth appears as the great principle of continuity for the people of God and as the means by which all kinds of men and women "from every tribe and tongue and people and nation" become part of God's people in Christ.

What about those who are not part of God's people in Christ in any conscious or explicit way? The New Testament writers hoped for a time in which all people would recognize the decisive significance of Christ within God's plan of salvation. They viewed Christ as the savior of the people of God and showed little interest in other possible ways of salvation. This apparent insularity was due in large part to early Christianity's eschatological orientation ("this world is passing away") and to the narrow geographical outlook of those who inhabited the lands around the Mediterranean Sea at the turn of the common era. The idea of universal salvation (universalism) is foreign to the New Testament, but the notion that all who do not make an explicit profession of faith in Jesus Christ are condemned (damnationism) is not championed either. The ultimate fate of nonbelievers is left in the hands of God.[3] However, the references to the cosmic significance of Christ's saving action in Paul's letters (see 2 Cor. 5:19; Rom. 8:19–23; 11:15) and in the Letters to the Colossians (see 1:20; 2:10, 15) and the Ephesians (see 1:10, 20–22; 3:10) may furnish some New Testament foundation for the inclusion within God's special people of those who remain "anonymous Christians" (to use Karl Rahner's somewhat infelicitous phrase).[4]

3. The communal significance of baptism. Baptism into Christ is the way by which we become part of God's people here and now. Many Jewish groups of Jesus' time practiced ritual washings of various sorts, but the distinctive feature about Christian baptism was its power to incorporate one into the body of Christ. In Rom. 6:3–4 baptism is portrayed as identification with the decisive events of Christ's life: "Do you not know that all of us who have been baptized into Christ Jesus were baptized into his death? We were buried therefore with him by baptism into death, so that as Christ was raised from the dead by the glory of the Father, we too might walk in newness of life." Galatians 3 states that "as many of you as were baptized into Christ have put on Christ" (v. 27) and that being "Christ's" makes us Abraham's offspring and heirs according to the promise. The rite of baptism obviously presupposes faith in the decisive significance of Jesus' life, death, and resurrection.[5] Consideration of how all of us—whatever our ethnic origins—become part of God's people reminds us that faith in Christ holds us together and helps us to appreciate the seriousness of our baptism. The long-standing debate about the appropriateness of infant baptism may never be resolved, but that debate should not be carried on as if the only alternatives were the informed personal commitment that only an adult can give and the desire to "cleanse" the infant from original sin. The importance of belonging to the community of faith is a factor too, and the communal dimension of salvation that emerges from understanding the church as God's people in Christ must not be overlooked. Baptism into Christ makes us members of God's people in Christ.

4. Christians as "honorary Jews." The Jewish roots of our Christian faith must be celebrated and not denied. The structure of faith after the pattern of Abraham—divinely initiated, historical, covenantal—is normative for the church. The Old Testament Scriptures must be proclaimed within the church, for they become fully intelligible according to Paul and the other New Testament authors only in the person of Jesus. In Romans 9—11 Paul shows that in a real sense we Gentile Christians are honorary Jews.[6] Paul could not conceive of the church as God's people in Christ without its having some relationship to Israel after the flesh. In the terms of Paul's parable, we Gentile Christians have been grafted onto the olive tree which is Israel. Even those New Testament books that engage in what is sometimes called "replacement theology" (that is, the church replaces Israel as God's people) exhibit a very serious interest in Israel's spiritual heritage. For example, the author of Hebrews takes the Exodus generation's wandering in the wilderness as a warning to the Christian community in 3:7—4:11, and the author of Revelation encourages his community in its crisis by reminding it of its status as priests of God. The church today cannot allow its Jewish past to be ignored, for without that past there is no validity to its claim to be God's people in Christ.

5. The scandal of anti-Semitism. The church must be on guard against anti-Semitism.[7] The church's claim to carry on the spiritual heritage of Israel has all too often provided individuals and groups with "theological" justifications for persecuting those Jews who maintain "the old ways." But the biblical evidence for the church's claim to be the people of God points in another direction. All the New Testament authors were conscious of their Jewish spiritual roots, and Paul was convinced that there was still a place for unbelieving Israel within God's plan of salvation. Furthermore, attention to the particular historical settings of the Gospels of Matthew and John shows that the most blatant "anti-Jewish" statements in the New Testament come from Jewish Christians speaking to predominantly Jewish-Christian churches engaged in a conflict

with other Jews claiming to be God's people. To equate "the scribes and Pharisees" in Matthew and "the Jews" in John with all Jews of our time is anachronistic and ahistorical lunacy. That is not to deny that a great deal of such lunacy has taken place and still exists. But it seems to be more imperative than ever that pastors and church leaders today carry out their solemn obligation to teach God's people in Christ to read the Scriptures intelligently. When the statements about Jews in Matthew and John are read with no concern for their historical setting and original meaning, the church continues to encourage a very dark and dangerous facet of Western civilization.

The unbelief of Israel remained a mystery to Paul, and it remains such to the church today. But that is no justification for all the pathetic and barbarous attempts throughout the ages at rooting out Israel. These acts are only a source of shame to those who now claim to be God's people in Christ. Moreover, Paul reserved a place for "unbelieving Israel" within the economy of salvation and left it to God to bring his plan to its fulfillment. Of course, this should not prevent Christians from wanting to share their religious vision and fellowship with Jews today. To withhold from another what one perceives as a precious spiritual treasure is selfishness, and selfishness is never very admirable. But Paul's conviction that Israel has a place in God's plan also challenges Christian theologians today to think about the possibility of finding a positive significance in the continued existence of Judaism. To go on using Judaism as the "left hand" of Christian faith or even to be satisfied with including the Jews in Rahner's mass of "anonymous Christians" do not seem to be adequate responses. The positive significance of Judaism is a topic just beginning to surface in discussions between Christian theologians and their Jewish counterparts. For Christians, the question is this: What positive contribution to Christian faith today can be made by Judaism as an independent group that carries on the heritage of ancient Israel? It is too early to know what answers will come out of such discussions, but the question is surely an important one.

6. Unity within the people of God. In Christ the ethnic, social, and sexual differences between persons become relatively unimportant. So in Gal. 3:28 Paul asserts, "There is neither Jew nor Greek, there is neither slave nor free, there is neither male nor female; for you are all one in Christ Jesus." The author of Ephesians picks up this theme in 2:14: "For he is our peace, who has made us both one, and has broken down the dividing wall of hostility." These texts do not say that the physical and social differences between people have ceased to exist entirely. The biblical writers were not that naive. But they do maintain that these distinctions are no longer terribly important. Frequently texts like Gal. 3:28 and Eph. 2:14 are used as slogans for radical social change or as justifications for social inertia. But their more fundamental thrust is neither change nor inertia. Rather, their more fundamental thrust is to make us appreciate the awesome change that occurs in baptism and the attitudes that ought to prevail within the community of baptized Christians. Prescinding for the moment from those outside the Christian community, we Christians cannot afford to let ethnic, social, or sexual distinctions be the sole criteria for action or inaction within the church. Every baptized Christian has the same awesome dignity before God, and every baptized Christian as part of God's people deserves our highest respect. On the other hand, prejudices against other Christians and violence between Christians totally contradict the church's identity as God's people in Christ.[8]

7. The people's pilgrimage. The people of God is a pilgrim people seeking its way in the world and journeying toward rest with God. In Romans 9—11 Paul made an effort to discern the flow of God's plan for humanity and the church's place in it. He firmly believed that God was using the church composed of Jews and Gentiles for his own good and creative purposes. The author of Hebrews warned his community to avoid the lack of trust and the disobedience that characterized

the Exodus generation's wandering in the wilderness. The history of the early churches is the story of minority groups finding their ways in a disinterested or even positively hostile environment. First Peter and Revelation illustrate that fact quite dramatically. The experiences of those churches that are captured in the foundational documents of the church should provide encouragement today not only for communities in places where Christians are few and the churches suffer organized persecution but also in places like America and western Europe where many of the church's cultural props are being removed and institutional change is proceeding at a dizzying pace. God's people in Christ is on a journey and cannot control everything that happens along the way. God himself is its guide and its goal, and fidelity to God is the only security available to God's people in Christ.

NOTES

1. G. Lohfink, *Die Sammlung Israels: Eine Untersuchung zur lukanischen Ekklesiologie*, SANT 39 (Munich: Kösel, 1975).

2. G. S. Sloyan, *Jesus on Trial: The Development of the Passion Narratives and Their Historical and Ecumenical Implications* (Philadelphia: Fortress Press, 1973). See also J. R. Donahue, *Are You the Christ? The Trial Narrative in the Gospel of Mark*, SBLDS 10 (Cambridge, Mass.: Society of Biblical Literature, 1973).

3. J. A. Burgess, "Approaches to the Question of Universal Salvation on the Basis of the New Testament," *Ohio Journal of Religious Studies* 5 (1977): 142–48.

4. K. Rahner, "Anonymous Christians," in *Theological Investigations Volume VI: Concerning Vatican Council II*, trans. K.-H. and B. Kruger (London: Darton, Longman & Todd, 1969; New York: Seabury Press), pp. 390–98. Rahner's effort at grounding the idea of anonymous Christians in 1 Tim. 2:4 ("who [God] desires all to be saved and to come to the knowledge of the truth") prescinds from the fact that in the pastorals the expression "the knowledge of the truth" (see also 2 Tim. 2:25; 3:7; Titus 1:1) is a formula for Christianity; that is, conversion to the Christian faith. See M. Dibelius and H. Conzelmann, *The Pastoral Epistles*, Hermeneia (Philadelphia: Fortress Press, 1972), p. 41.

5. D. J. Harrington, "Baptism in the Spirit: A Review Article," *Chicago Studies* 11 (1972): 31–44.

6. K. Stendahl, *Paul Among Jews and Gentiles and Other Essays* (Philadelphia: Fortress Press, 1976).

7. S. Sandmel, *Anti-Semitism in the New Testament?* (Philadelphia: Fortress Press, 1978). See also E. J. Fisher, *Faith without Prejudice: Rebuilding Christian Attitudes toward Judaism* (New York, Ramsey, and Toronto: Paulist Press, 1977).

8. W. Rader, *The Church and Racial Hostility: A History of Interpretation of Ephesians 2:11–22*, BGBE 20 (Tübingen: Mohr-Siebeck, 1978).

Suggestions for
Further Reading

Hare, D. R. A. *The Theme of Jewish Persecution of Christians in the Gospel according to St. Matthew.* SNTSMS 6. New York and London: Cambridge University Press, 1967. This book not only assembles the evidence regarding the conflicts between Jews and Christians in the first century and beyond but also provides an excellent redaction-critical analysis of the references to Jewish persecution of Christians in Matthew's Gospel. Hare concludes that Matthew located the continuity between the two periods of salvation history in the Messiah, not in the people of God.

Klein, C. *Anti-Judaism in Christian Theology.* Translated by E. Quinn. Philadelphia: Fortress Press, 1978. Concerned primarily with manifestations of anti-Judaism in German New Testament scholarship during the past fifty years, the author shows how deep and persistent the negative evaluation of Judaism has been in Christian theology. Her own understanding of first-century Judaism, however, is open to objections, since it is based almost entirely on rabbinic sources.

Kraus, H. J. *The People of God in the Old Testament.* New York and London: Association Press, 1958. A concise presentation of how Israel's understanding of itself as God's people developed against the background of its history. Kraus, a German Old Testament specialist, is well known for his research on the cultic dimensions of Israelite religion.

Küng, H. *The Church*. London: Burns and Oates, 1967; Garden City, N.Y.: Doubleday & Co., Image Books, 1976. An extraordinarily successful blend of biblical exegesis, historical information, and theological thinking. For a general understanding of modern viewpoints in ecclesiology, there is no better starting point. The section on the church as the people of God, however, is not the strongest part of the book.

Richardson, P. *Israel in the Apostolic Church*. SNTSMS 10. New York and London: Cambridge University Press, 1970. How did Christians come to adopt Jewish prerogatives and attributes, and in particular, how did the church come to assume the name "Israel"? The author maintains that this was a long process and that it was not until the time of Justin Martyr (mid-second century) that the equation between the church and the "true Israel" was made.

Sanders, E. P. *Paul and Palestinian Judaism: A Comparison of Patterns of Religion*. Philadelphia: Fortress Press, 1977. Hailed by S. Sandmel as one of the very great works of New Testament scholarship in our time, this study argues that by consistently maintaining the basic framework of covenant nomism, Palestinian Jews kept the gift and demand of God in a healthy relationship and observed the minute points of the Law on the basis of the large principles of religion. The author also claims that Paul presents an essentially different type of righteousness from any found in Palestinian Jewish literature.

Sandmel, S. *Anti-Semitism in the New Testament?* Philadelphia: Fortress Press, 1978. Using the term *anti-Semitism* in somewhat loose fashion, a very distinguished Jewish scholar urges Christians to recognize the elements of anti-Semitism within the New Testament writings and asks whether this is a permanent and irremovable aspect of Christianity.

Sevenster, J. N. *The Roots of Pagan Anti-Semitism in the Ancient World*. NovTSup 41. Leiden: Brill, 1975. The author explores some of the root causes proposed as explanations for pagan anti-Semitism in antiquity: racial distinctiveness, social status, strangeness, and politics. While admitting that a great diversity of opinions regarding Judaism existed in antiquity, he concludes that the deepest reason for pagan anti-Semitism lay in the offense caused by the strangeness of Jews in ancient society. The book is a very useful synthesis.

Sloyan, G. S. *Is Christ the End of the Law?* Biblical Perspectives on Current Issues. Philadelphia: Westminster Press, 1978. Prominent for many years in Christian-Jewish dialogue, the author is concerned here with the relationship between the covenant Law delivered to the Hebrew people and God's gracious action in Jesus Christ. He concludes that Christ is the end of the Law as its completion rather than as its abrogation and that Christianity today should be true to its oldest traditions on this matter.

Stendahl, K. *Paul Among Jews and Gentiles and Other Essays.* Philadelphia: Fortress Press, 1976. The title essay, which constitutes more than half the book, contends that the relation between Jews and Gentiles was a primary factor in shaping Paul's thought and action. The article on Paul and the introspective consciousness of the West has become a classic in New Testament study.

Indexes

AUTHORS, EDITORS, AND TRANSLATORS

123

SCRIPTURE REFERENCES

EARLY JEWISH SOURCES